Second Japanese Reader:

A Dual-Language Book for Progressing from Beginning to Intermediate Japanese

Copyright © 2017

All rights reserved.

CONTENTS

PREFACE

In order to make language learning logical and simple, the reading material in textbooks is usually quite dull. And most textbooks don't teach much about the writing style of novels and short stories. This means that even an intermediate student of Japanese might encounter many difficulties when attempting to explore Japanese literature. This book is aimed at students who wish to bridge this gap between real Japanese literature and the reading material of textbooks.

This book will also help students learn or solidify a lot of the grammar found in level N4 of the Japanese Language Proficiency Test and introduce them to some of the grammar in level N3. It will also help to expand their vocabulary, because while the stories in this collection are based on stories from Japanese folklore, they have been written in a more accessible manner and with common words.

Each story is presented first in Japanese followed by an English translation. Yet, the English version is more literal than might be found in a stand-alone translation in order to help the reader better understand its connection with the Japanese.

Following this, the story will be divided into smaller sections where each new word is defined and explanations of the grammar involved are given. However, this is a continuation of the first book, so extremely common words like 言う and 思う as well as elementary particles will not be defined, nor will there be explanations for the grammar that was covered in the first book. And again in this book, explanations of each aspect of grammar will also only be given once and the stories become progressively more difficult, so the reader is encouraged to read them in order.

Also, to better prepare you for progressing to an intermediate level, no translation has been provided for the final story. However, all of the grammar in the story has already been covered and most of the words have already been seen, although there is still a vocabulary section.

SECOND JAPANESE READER

浦島太郎

　昔々、海辺の村に、浦島太郎という若い漁師がお母さんと二人で暮らしていました。ある日、浦島太郎が浜を歩いていると、子供たちが亀をいじめているのを見ました。。「なんてひどいことを」とかわいそうに思い、逃がしてやるように子供たちに「これこれ、その亀をほうっておいてくれ」と要求しました。

　「いやだよ。僕たちがやっと捕まえたんだもの。どうしようと、僕たちの勝手だろ」と子供たちは叩いたりけったりしながら言いました。

　見ると亀は涙をハラハラとこぼしながら、浦島太郎を見つめていました。

　「どうするつもりだ」

　「町へ売りに行く」と一番年上の子供が言いました。

　「そんならわしにゆずっておくれ」と、お金を取り出すと、子供たちに差し出して言いました。

　「うん、それならいいよ」

　そこで、持っていたわずかばかりのお金を渡して亀を助けてやりました。

　子供たちから亀を受け取ると、「大丈夫かい？もう、二度と捕まるんじゃないぞ」と、亀をそっと、海の中に逃がしてやりました。亀はうれしそうに首を振っていましたが、やがて波の中へ消えていきました。

　それから数日経って、浦島太郎が海で釣りをしていると、誰かが声をかけてきました。
　「浦島さん、浦島さん...」
　「おや、誰が呼んでいるのだろう？」
　「私ですよ」
　すると海の上に、突然亀が頭を出して言いました。
　浦島太郎はびっくりして亀を見ました。
　「この間は助けていただいて、ありがとうございました」
と、亀は浦島太郎に感謝の言葉を述べた。
　「ああ、あの時のカメさん」
　「はい、お礼に竜宮へ案内します。私の背中に乗ってください」
言うなり、亀は大きくなりました。
　「竜宮？さあ、竜宮って、どこにあるんだい？」と、浦島太郎は疑わしそうに大きな亀を見つめながら、言った。
　「海の底です」
　「えっ！海の底へなんか、行けるのかい？」
　「はい。私がお連れしましょう。さあ、背中へ乗ってください」
　亀は浦島太郎を乗せて、海の中にずんずんともぐっていきました。
　海の中には真っ青な光が差し込み、コンブがユラユラと揺れ、赤とピンクのサンゴの林がどこまでも続けています。浦島太郎はうっとりしていると、あっという間に立派な門がある城に着きました。屋根には金のかわらが並び、壁は銀でできていました。
　「到着しましたよ。このお城が竜宮城です。さあ、こちらへ」
　門をくぐると、乙姫様がたくさんの女の人たちと一緒にお城へ出てきました。
　（なんてきれいな人だ。）
　「ようこそ、浦島さん。私はこの竜宮の主人の乙姫です。この間は亀を助けてくださって、ありがとうございます。

お礼に竜宮をご案内します。どうぞ、ゆっくりしていってください ね」と、乙姫様は鈴の鳴るような声で言いました。

あまりの美しさに驚いて浦島太郎は声も出ません。

浦島太郎は竜宮の広間へ案内されました。床は実に美しい色合いの大理石でできていて、部屋の中央に大きなテーブルがありました。テーブルの上に山のようなごちそうが並んでいます。

浦島太郎が用意された席に座ると、魚たちが次から次へと素晴らしいごちそうを運んできます。

「さあ、めしあがれ」

乙姫様はお酒を注いでくれました。こんな美味しい酒は飲んだことがありません。

ふんわりと気持ちの良い音楽が流れて、タイやヒラメたちの舞いや踊りを見ながらたくさんのごちそうを食べてしばらく楽しい時を過ごしました。やがて、何もかも忘れてうっとりと眺めました。

まるで夢のような毎日が過ぎていきました。何日か過ぎると、ある日浦島太郎はふと、お母さんのことに思い出しました。その途端、急に家が恋しくなりました。そこで、乙姫様に言いました。

「今までありがとうございます。長い間お世話になりましたが、そろそろ家へ帰らせていただきます」

「帰られるのですか？いつまでもあなたと一緒に暮らしていたかったのに」

「いいえ、私の帰りを待つ者もおりますので」

すると乙姫様が寂しそうに言いました。

「...そうですか。仕方ありません。では、お土産に玉手箱を差し上げましょう」

「玉手箱？」

「はい。この中には、浦島さんが竜宮で過ごされた『時』が入っております。これを開けずに持っている限り、浦島さんは年を取りません。ずっと、今の若い姿のままでいられます。ですが一度開けてしまうと、今までの『時』が戻ってしまいますので、どんなことがあっても決して開けてはいけませんよ」

「わかりました。乙姫様の親切は一生忘れません」

浦島太郎は喜んで玉手箱をもらいました。

「それでは私の背中に乗ってください」と、亀が出てきて言いました。

浦島太郎は玉手箱を抱えて亀の背中に乗って、あっという間に故郷の浜に着きました。

しかし，何とかそこは以前の村とは違っているように思えました。周辺を歩いてみたのですが、誰も知っている者がいないのです。慌てて自分の家の方へ駆けていきました。しかし、自分の家があった辺りには草が生えていて、家もなく、母の姿も見えません。

「わたしの家は、どうなったのだろう？　みんなはどこかへ、引っ越したのだろうか？」

でも、出会った人に尋ねても誰も家のことを知らないのです。浦島太郎はすっかり変わってしまった村のあちこちを歩き回りました。でも、知っている人は一人もいなく、家のことや母のことを尋ねても首を傾げるばかりです。

「あの、すみません。浦島の家を知りませんか？」

浦島太郎が一人の老人に尋ねてみると、老人は少し首を傾げて言いました。

「浦島？　・・・ああ、たしか浦島という人なら三百年ほど前に海へ出たまま帰らないそうですよ」

「えっ！？」

老人の話しを聞いて、浦島太郎はびっくり。

わずか一年ほど竜宮で暮らしたと思っていたのに、本当は三百年も経っていたのです。竜宮の一年は、この世の三百年にあたるのでしょうか？

（そんなばかかな。）

「家族も友だちも、みんな死んでしまったのか・・・」

浦島太郎は玉手箱を抱えて、海辺へ戻ってきました。昔と変わらないのは海の景色だけです。

　がっくりと肩を落とした浦島太郎は、ふと、持っていた玉手箱を見つめました。

　「そう言えば、乙姫様は言っていたな。この玉手箱を開けると、『時』が戻ってしまうと。・・・もしかしてこれを開けると、自分が暮らしていた時に戻るのでは」

　そう思った浦島太郎は、開けてはいけないと言われていた玉手箱を開けてしまいました。

　すると中から、真っ白の煙は出てきました。

　煙の中に、竜宮や美しい乙姫様の姿が映りました。

　そして楽しかった竜宮での一年が、次から次へと映し出されます。浦島太郎は、喜びました。

　でも玉手箱から出てきた煙は次第に薄れていき、その場に残ったのは髪が真っ白なおじいさんになった浦島太郎だったのです。

TARO URASHIMA

Long, long ago, in a seaside village, there lived a young fisherman named Taro Urashima together with his mother. One day, Taro Urashima was walking along the beach when he saw some children pestering a turtle.

"How cruel," he thought pityingly, and in order to set it free, he demanded to the children, "Hey! Leave the turtle alone!"

"No way, we finally caught it, so we can do whatever we want with it," the children said while hitting and kicking it.

Taro Urashima saw the turtle staring at him while shedding tears rapidly in large drops.

"What do you intend to do with it?"

"We're going to town to sell it," the oldest boy said.

"In that case, please turn it over to me," he said and took out some money which he offered to the boys.

"Alright then."

So he handed over what little money he had and saved the turtle.

When he claimed the turtle from the children, he said, "Are you alright? Now, don't get caught a second time," and let the turtle loose in the sea. The turtle shook his head cheerfully and soon disappeared beneath the waves.

After that, many days passed and then a voice spoke to him while Taro Urashima was fishing.

"Mr. Urashima, Mr. Urashima…"

"Huh, who is calling me?"

"It's me."

The turtle suddenly said as it poked its head above the waves.

Taro Urashima looked at the turtle in surprise.

"Thank you very much for rescuing me the other day," the turtle expressed its thanks to Taro Urashima.

"Oh, you are the turtle from then."

"Yes, I am the turtle whom you saved. In thanks, I will guide you to the Palace of the Dragon King. Please climb aboard my back."

As soon as the turtle said this, it grew large.

"The Palace of the Dragon King? Hmm…well where is this Palace of the Dragon King?" Taro Urashima said while gazing dubiously at the large turtle.

"It's at the bottom of the sea."

"What? Can we go all the way to the bottom of the sea?"

"Yes. Allow me to take you. Now please climb aboard my back."

The turtle took Taro Urashima on board and then plunged into the sea.

A deep blue light shined in the sea, the seaweed gently swayed to and fro, and the forest of pink and red coral went on endlessly. Taro Urashima was enthralled and arrived in the blink of an eye at the castle where there was an elegant gate. On the roof of the castle golden tiles were laid, and the walls were made of silver.

"We have arrived. This castle is the Palace of the Dragon King."

When they passed beneath the gate, Lady Otohime came out of the castle together with many other women.

(What a beautiful person.)

"Welcome, Mr. Urashima. I am Otohime, the proprietress of the Palace of the Dragon King. I thank you for helping the turtle the other day. Out of gratitude, I will show you around the Palace of the Dragon King. Please make yourself comfortable." Lady Otohime said in a voice that rang like a bell.

Such was her beauty that Taro Urashima was overwhelmed and couldn't speak.

Urashima was shown to the Hall in the Palace of the Dragon King. The floor was made of marble of a truly beautiful hue and there was a large table in the center of the room on top of which a mountainous feast was spread.

Taro Urashima sat in the prepared seat and, one after another, the fish carried the magnificent feast to him.

"Eat!"

Lady Otohime poured sake for him. Such delicious sake he had never before drank.

Pleasant music flowed airily and he spent quite a while enjoying the abundant feast as he watched the sea bream and flounder whirl and dance. Before long, he forgot all else and stared in a trance.

Every day passed as though it were a dream. After some number of days had passed, one day out of the blue Taro Urashima recalled various things about his mother. At that moment, he suddenly became homesick.

So he said to Lady Otohime, "I thank you for everything you've done. You have taken care of me for a long time, but please allow me to go home now."

"You're going to leave me? I wanted to live with you forever..."

"I can't, there are people waiting on my return."

Then Lady Otohime said forlornly, "Is that so. If you must, then I will give you a *tamate* box as a parting gift."

"*Tamate* box?"

"It will hold the "time" that you spent in the Palace of the Dragon King inside it. As long as you keep it without opening it, you will not age. You will be able to stay in your present young form forever. But once you open it, the "time" up to then will return, so no matter what happens you must never open it."

"I understand. I will not forget your kindness for the rest of my life."

Taro Urashima received the *tamate* box gladly.

"Well then, please climb aboard my back," the turtle appeared and said.

Carrying the *tamate* box, Taro Urashima got on the turtle's back and, before he knew it, he had arrived at the beach of his hometown.

But the village seemed somewhat different from before. He took a walk in the vicinity but there was no one he knew. In a panic, he ran toward his house. However, grass was growing in the area where his house had been, and not only was there no house, his mother was also nowhere to be seen.

"What became of my house? Did everyone move away somewhere?"

But even when he asked the people he happened to meet, no one knew anything about his house. Taro Urashima walked around, here and there, in this town that had completely changed. And there wasn't a single person he knew and even if he asked about his mother and his house, they all just tilted their heads.

"Um, excuse me. Do you know the Urashima family?"

Taro Urashima asked an old man, and the old man tilted his head slightly to the side, saying,

"Urashima?...Oh, if I remember correctly, it's said that there was a person named Urashima who disappeared into the sea and never returned home."

"What!"

Taro Urashima was shocked to hear what the man said.

He thought he had lived for only a year in the Palace of the Dragon King, but in truth three hundred years had passed. Is it that one year in the Palace of the Dragon King corresponds to three hundred years in the world?

(That's ridiculous.)

"My family, friends, has everyone died...?"

Taro Urashima returned to the beach carrying the *tamate* box. The only thing that had not changed was the seascape. He didn't know what he should do. With his shoulders drooping despondently, Taro Urashima suddenly gazed at the *tamate* box he held.

"That reminds me of what Lady Otohime said. That if I open the *tamate* box, "time" will return. Perhaps if I open it, I will return to the time that I lived..."

Thinking so, Taro Urashima opened the *tamate* box he had been told that he shouldn't open. And from inside, pure white smoke came forth.

In the smoke, he saw the Palace of the Dragon King, the beautiful Lady Otohime, and various other scenes. And the pleasant year in the Palace of the Dragon King played out in succession. Taro Urashima was delighted.

But the smoke that came out from the *tamate* box gradually thinned and what remained in its place was the bent-backed old man with stark white hair and beard that Taro Urashima had become.

VOCABULARY AND GLOSS

　昔々、海辺の村に、浦島太郎という若い漁師がお母さんと二人で暮らしていました。ある日，浦島太郎が浜を歩いていると、子供たちが亀をいじめているのを見ました。「なんてひどいことを」とかわいそうに思い、逃がしてやるように子供たちに「これこれ、その亀をほうっておいてくれ」と要求しました。

浦島太郎【うらしまたろう】Taro Urashima
海辺【うみべ】Beach, seashore
漁師【りょうし】Fisherman
暮らす【くらす】To live
浜【はま】Beach
亀【かめ】Turtle
いじめる　To torment
ひどい　Cruel, heartless
逃がす【にがす】To set free
ほうっておく　To leave (object) alone
要求【ようきゅう】Demand, firm request

The use here of ように in the last sentence does not mean "like," it is used to express a desire or wish and so is usually translated as "so that" or "in order to." In fact, ように can be used to turn a sentence into a wish when it comes at the end of a sentence in ます-form:

二人が幸せでありますように！

May you both be happy!

　「いやだよ。僕たちがやっと捕まえたんだもの。何をしようと、僕たちの勝手だろう」と子供たちは叩いたりけったりしながら言いました。

　見ると亀は涙をハラハラとこぼしながら、浦島太郎を見つめていました。

　「何をするつもりだ」

　「町へ売りに行く」と一番年上の子供が言いました。

　「それならわしにゆずっておくれ」と、お金を取り出すと、子供たちに差し出して言いました。

　「うん、それならいいよ」

いやだ　No way, not a chance

僕【ぼく】I (male casual form)

やっと　Finally, at last

捕まえる【つかまえる】To capture

何をしようと　*See below

勝手【かって】As (I) like

叩く【たたく】To slap, beat

ける　To kick

ハラハラと　Falling rapidly in big drops

こぼす　To shed (tears)

見つめる【みつめる】To gaze at

年上【としうえ】Older

それなら　If that's the case

わし I (old male casual form)

ゆずる to turn over

At the end of sentences, もの has a few different meanings, but here it is used to give a reason for what precedes it. The copula だ has been dropped as is often the case when this ending is used in conversational Japanese.

何をしよう is the volitional form of 何をする and 何をしようと has the same meaning as 何をするとしても (としても

means "even if" and when paired with a wh-word (like 何), it takes on the meaning "no matter (what)…"). Thus the phrase 何をしようと is used here to mean, "No matter what (we) will do." 僕たちの勝手 is a phrase meaning "as we like."

何をしようと、私の勝手でしょう is actually a phrase that is commonly used with people who are not close friends when you'd prefer not to talk about something. It's a polite way of saying, "It's none of your business." or "I'd prefer to talk about something else." Therefore, this is a good phrase to memorize.

たり is like the や of て-form. So while 叩いて、ける means hit and kick, 叩いたりけったりする means that they also did other unlisted things besides hitting and kicking. In proper grammar, the last たり is followed by する; however, this can also be dropped in conversational Japanese.

"お+" imperative form is a soft imperative form. Imperative forms are used to issue commands and orders (for most verbs, this means changing the final "u" to "e"). For example, やめ！ means, "Stop!" Imperative forms are used a lot in anime and manga, but in real life, people tend to use the more polite なさい-form. So when Urashima says, ゆずっておくれ, he is issuing a polite command to the children to sell the turtle to him instead of bringing it to town.

　そこで，持っていたわずかばかりのお金を渡して亀を助けてやりました。
　子供たちから亀を受け取ると、「大丈夫かい？もう、二度と捕まるんじゃないぞ」と、亀をそっと、海の中に逃がしてやりました。亀はうれしそうに首を振っていましたが、やがて波の中へ消えていきました。

そこで　So, accordingly
わずか　Small quantity
ばかり　Only
渡す【わたす】To hand over
助ける【たすける】To rescue, save
受け取る【うけとる】To receive
もう　Anymore, again
二度【にど】Twice, again
捕まる【つかまる】Gets captured
そっと　Quietly, gently, softly
海【うみ】The sea
うれしい　Glad
首を振る【くびをふる】To shake one's head
やがて　Soon, before long
波【なみ】Waves
消える【きえる】To vanish

The phrase 持っていたわずかばかりのお金 might seem a little confusing at first because お金 has two modifiers: 持っていた and わずかばかりの. Since noun modifiers almost always come before the noun in Japanese, this bunching up happens quite frequently and is just something that we need to get used to.

The question particle かい can replace the particle か at the end of sentences, but is only used for yes/no questions.

Strangely, sometimes the word 首 is used to mean head in Japanese, so we need to pay attention to context with this word. (This usage happens again later in the story.) And が can often be translated as "but," however, in some cases it functions more like "and" as it does in the last sentence here.

　それから数日経って、浦島太郎が海で釣りをしていると、誰かが声をかけてきました。
　「浦島さん、浦島さん…」
　「おや、誰が呼んでいるのだろう？」
　「私ですよ」
　すると海の上に、突然亀が頭を出して言いました。
　浦島太郎はびっくりして亀を見ました。
　「この間は助けていただいて、ありがとうございました」
と、亀は浦島太郎に感謝の言葉を述べた。
　「ああ、あの時のカメさん」
　「はい、お礼に竜宮へ案内します。私の背中に乗ってください」
　言うなり、亀は大きくなりました。

数日【すうじつ】A few days
経つ【たつ】To pass, lapse
釣り【つり】Fishing
声【こえ】をかける　To call out, greet
おや　Oh!
呼ぶ【よぶ】To call out
のだろう？　I wonder…
すると　Whereupon
突然【とつぜん】Suddenly, unexpectedly
頭【あたま】Head
出す【だす】To reveal, present

びっくりする　Is surprised
この間【このあいだ】The other day
感謝【かんしゃ】Thanks, gratitude
言葉【ことば】Words
述べる【のべる】To state, express
お礼【おれい】Expression of gratitude
竜宮【りゅうぐう】Palace of the Dragon King
案内【あんない】To guide
背中【せなか】Back (of body)
乗る【のる】To board, get on
〜なり　As soon as

いただく is a politer version of もらう, so 助けていただく means "I received your help."

ありがとうございました is exactly what it looks like: the past tense of ありがとうございます. There is no past tense of "thank you" in English, so this takes some getting used to, but a good example involves getting a ride from someone. If you thank the person during the ride, you use present tense and if you thank them when they drop you off, you use past tense. This is the reason why when you pay for something at a store, the clerks will say ありがとうございました as you walk away; because they are thanking you for the purchase, which is in the past. However, people often use the present tense at both times, so when in doubt, just use ありがとうございます.

When なり follows the dictionary form of a verb, it has the meaning, "as soon as" or "right after." So 言うなり means, "right after (the turtle) said (this)…"

　「竜宮？さあ、竜宮って、どこにあるんだい？」と、浦島太郎は疑わしそうに大きな亀を見つめながら、言った。
　「海の底です」
　「えっ！海の底へなんか、行けるのかい？」
　「はい。私がお連れしましょう。さあ、背中へ乗ってください」
　亀は浦島太郎を乗せて、海の中にずんずんともぐっていきました。

疑わしい【うたがわしい】Doubtful, uncertain
底【そこ】The bottom
連れる【つれる】To take (a person)
乗せる【のせる】To give (someone) a ride
ずんずん　Rapidly
もぐる　To dive

The sentence ending particle だい can be used in place of the question particle か when the question is a wh-question, but only in casual conversation. Notice that the turtle uses very polite language and Urashima speaks casually, presumably because Urashima is human and the turtle is not. For example the turtle uses keigo in the second to last sentence: お連れしましょう. When speaking to a 目上【めうえ】 "a social superior," most verbs can be conjugated as "お+ the ます-stem of a verb + する" to show respect to that person. And as in the story 雪女, the volitional form is used here to express an intention or determination.

なんか is often attached to words to emphasize them in order to express an emotion or to belittle something. For example, 雪なんかきらいだ！ "I hate snow!" It can sometimes be translated as "or something like that," but often some other alternative needs to be found in English. When Urashima uses it, he is emphasizing "to the bottom of the sea" because he is in disbelief, thus the translation reads, "all the way." In some parts of Japan, なんか is also used in place of ええと, "um," when people are thinking of what to say, which can sometimes be confusing.

　海の中には真っ青な光が差し込み、コンブがユラユラと揺れ、赤とピンクのサンゴの林がどこまでも続けています。浦島太郎はうっとりしていると、あっという間に立派な門がある城に着きました。屋根には金のかわらが並び、壁は銀でできていました。

真っ青な【まっさおな】Deep blue
光【ひかり】Light
差し込む【さしこむ】To shine in
コンブ　Kelp
フラフラ　Swaying
揺れる【ゆれる】To sway
赤【あか】Red
ピンク　Pink
サンゴ　Coral
林【はやし】Forest, thicket
どこまでも　Everywhere, thoroughly
続ける【つづける】To continue
うっとりする　Is entranced
あっという間【ま】The blink of an eye
立派【りっぱ】Splendid, elegant
門【もん】Gate
城【しろ】Castle
着く【つく】To arrive at
屋根【やね】Roof
金【きん】Gold

かわら　Roof tiles
並ぶ【ならぶ】To line up
壁【かべ】Wall
銀【ぎん】Silver
できる　To make

As we also saw in 雪女, the auxiliary verb 込む adds the meaning of "into" to the verb it is attached to, so 海の中に差し込む means, "to shine into the sea." The phrase あっという間に literally means, "in the time it takes to say 'ah!'" which might make its meaning easier to remember. The kanji 金 is one of several annoying kanji whose pronunciation depends on context: it is pronounced きん when it refers to gold, but かね when it means money.

Cultural Note:
銀座【ぎんざ】is an upscale shopping district in Tokyo that is known world-wide for its luxurious shops. The name comes from the area being a silver-coin mint during the Edo period.

And two famous sites in Kyoto are 金閣寺【きんかくじ】and 銀閣寺【ぎんかくじ】the Gold Pavilion and the Silver Pavilion. These were originally villas that have since been converted into Zen Buddhist temples. Both sites also contain very beautiful gardens.

「到着しましたよ。このお城が竜宮城です」
門をくぐると、乙姫様がたくさんの女の人たちと一緒にお城
へ出てきました。
　（なんてきれいな人だ。）
　「ようこそ、浦島さん。私はこの竜宮の主人の乙姫です。
この間は亀を助けてくださって、ありがとうございます。お
礼に竜宮をご案内します。どうぞ、ゆっくりしていってくだ
さいね」と、乙姫様は鈴の鳴るような声で言いました。
　あまりの美しさに驚いて浦島太郎は声も出ません。

到着【とうちゃく】To arrive
〜城【〜じょう】Castle (suffix)
くぐる　To pass under
〜様【さま】*see below
出る【でる】To come forth, appear
なんて　How…! What…!
きれい　Beautiful
ようこそ Welcome
主人【しゅじん】Head (of a household)
どうぞ　Please
ゆっくり　At ease, restful
鈴【すず】A bell
鳴る【なる】To ring
声【こえ】Voice
あまりの　Excess, too much
美しい【うつくしい】Beautiful
驚く【おどろく】Is surprised, astonished
声を出す【こえをだす】To speak

The name suffix 〜様 is a politer version of 〜さん and can be
added to some words to make them more polite. Often when a
receptionist asks your name they will say, どちら様ですか？

We saw in The Cat's Teacup that when なんて comes at the beginning of a sentence that contains some kind of description, it serves as an intensifier usually equivalent to saying, "How...! What...!" in English. For example, なんて面白い本！ "What an interesting book!"

くださる is the honorific form of くれる and carries the exact same meaning.

Just like we saw earlier, ご案内する is a form of keigo; most verbs which are a noun followed by する, like 案内, take ご instead of お.

By replacing an adjective's い-ending with さ, い- adjectives can be converted into nouns. So in this case, 美しい "beautiful" is changed into 美しさ "beauty."

浦島太郎は竜宮の広間へ案内されました。床は実に美しい色合いの大理石でできていて、部屋の中央に大きなテーブルがありました。テーブルの上に山のようなごちそうが並んでいます。

浦島太郎が用意された席に座ると、魚たちが次から次へと素晴らしいごちそうを運んできます。

「さあ、めしあがれ」

広間【ひろま】Hall, guest room
床【ゆか】Floor
実に【じつに】Truly, indeed
色合い【いろあい】Hue
大理石【だいりせき】Marble
中央【ちゅうおう】Center
大きな【おおきな】Large
ごちそう　Feast
用意【ようい】To prepare

席【せき】Seat
座る【すわる】To sit
魚【さかな】Fish
次【つぎ】から次へと　In succession
素晴らしい【すばらしい】Magnificent, splendid
運ぶ【はこぶ】To carry, transport
さあ Come on
めしあがる To eat

　〜たち is a pluralizing suffix, which you have probably used in 私たち. As English speakers, we may be tempted to overuse this suffix since Japanese nouns don't have a plural form. But don't go crazy with this suffix, if it's clear from context that something is plural, there's no need to add this suffix.

　In addition to "お+ the ます-stem of a verb + する," certain words can be replaced by "honorific forms" like めしあがる. This can be used instead of 食べる when speaking to a 目上 to show them respect. Here, it is in imperative form.

　乙姫様はお酒を注いでくれました。こんな美味しい酒を飲んだことはありません。

　ふんわりと気持ちが良い音楽が流れて、タイやヒラメたちの舞いや踊りを見ながらたくさんのごちそうを食べてしばらく楽しい時を過ごしました。やがて、何もかも忘れてうっとりと眺めました。

お酒【おさけ】Sake
注ぐ【そそぐ】To pour
こんな　Such
美味しい【おいしい】Delicious
ふんわり　Airily, fluffily
気持ちが良い【きもちがいい】Pleasant
音楽【おんがく】Music
流れる【ながれる】To flow
タイ　Sea bream
ヒラメ　Flounder
舞う【まう】To dance (whirling)
踊る【おどる】To dance (hopping)
しばらく A while
時を過ごす【ときをすごす】To spend time
何もかも【なにもかも】Anything and everything
忘れる【わすれる】To forget
うっとり　Absorbedly
眺める【ながめる】To stare

Verbs can be changed into nouns by putting them in ます-stem form with no ending as we see with 舞い and 踊り in the second sentence here. This of course won't work with all verbs, since some don't really make sense as a noun. Also, while 舞う and 踊る both mean to dance, 踊る is the more general word and 舞う is usually used to describe the dancing movement of cherry blossoms and leaves.

まるで夢のような毎日が過ぎていきました。何日か過ぎると、ある日浦島太郎はふと、お母さんのことに思い出しました。その途端、急に家が恋しくなりました。そこで、乙姫様に言いました。

「今までありがとうございます。長い間お世話になりましたが、そろそろ家へ帰らなくてはいけません」

まるで　As though, as if
夢【ゆめ】Dream
毎日【まいにち】Everyday
過ぎる【すぎる】To pass
何日か【なんにちか】Several days
ある日【あるひ】One day
ふと　Suddenly, unexpectedly
思い出す【おもいだす】To recall, remember
その途端【そのとたん】Just then
急に【きゅうに】Suddenly
家【いえ】House, family
恋しい【こいしい】Missed, yearned for
そこで　So, accordingly
今まで【いままで】Until now, so far
長い間【ながいあいだ】Long interval
お世話【せわ】になる　To receive favor
そろそろ　Now, It's about time

Saying お母さんのこと instead of just お母さん carries a subtly different meaning. Adding のこと is like saying, "all the things that are mom." It gives it more of a feeling of a universe of traits surrounding the noun instead of just the noun itself. This is often used with 好き. Like あなたのことが好き。 "I like everything that is you." or "I like everything about you." Clearly this can sometimes present difficulties in translation.

そろそろ is a very good word to know. It expresses that it is "about time" to do something, so it is often used as a way to end an activity, finish a phone call, leave someone's house, etc.

そろそろ家へ帰る時間だ。 It's about time I was going home.

The phrase 帰らなくてはいけません might look really complicated if you've never seen it before, especially since it has a double negative in it. But いけない is just a synonym of だめ, "no good, useless." It's like saying, "no go." The ては in this statement turns it into a conditional, so the phrase literally means, "If I don't return home, it's no good." The conclusion, then, is that one "must" return home, which is what なくてはいけません boils down to.

「帰られるのですか？いつまでもあなたと一緒に暮らしていたかったのに」

「いいえ、私の帰りを待つ者もおりますので」

すると乙姫様が寂しそうに言いました。

「...そうですか。仕方ありません。では、お土産に玉手箱を差し上げましょう」

「玉手箱？」

いつまでも Forever
者【もの】 Person, people
おる To be (Humble)
寂しい【さびしい】 Lonely
仕方ない【しかたない】 It can't be helped
では　Then, well
お土産【おみやげ】 Souvenir, present
玉手箱【たまてばこ】 Tamate box
差し上げる【さしあげる】 To give

Note that here Otohime is using the "inconvenienced" passive when she says 帰られる because she will suffer by his returning home. Even though the verb is "to return (where one belongs)," the implication is that he's going to be leaving her all alone, thus the translation.

のに is a conjunction similar to けど and が except のに expresses the speaker's attitude, conveying such feelings as resentment, envy, disappointment, and admiration. (This often can't be translated into English unless you use emojis.) Because the Japanese don't like to be direct, sentences often end with けど, が, and のに with the implication left unstated or stated beforehand as it is here.

おる is the humble version of いる and 差し上げる is the humble version of 上げる. Both Otohime and Urashima are speaking very politely to each other.

「はい。この中には、浦島さんが竜宮で過ごされた『時』が入っております。これを開けずに持っている限り、浦島さんは年を取りません。ずっと、今の若い姿のままでいられます。ですが一度開けてしまうと、今までの『時』が戻ってしまいますので、どんなことがあっても決して開けてはいけませんよ」
「わかりました。乙姫様の親切は一生忘れません」
浦島太郎は喜んで玉手箱をもらいました。

～ずに　Without doing…
限り【かぎり】As long as…
年を取る【としをとる】To age
ずっと　Continuously in some state
若い【わかい】Young
姿【すがた】Form, appearance
まま　As it is

ですが　But
一度【いちど】Once
戻る【もどる】To return
どんな　What (kind of)
決して【けっして】Never
わかった　Understood
親切【しんせつ】Kindness, gentleness
一生【いっしょう】Whole life
忘れる【わすれる】To forget
喜ぶ【よろこぶ】To be glad, delighted

〜ずに is a holdover from classical Japanese and has the same meaning as 〜ないで; however, 〜ずに is only used in writing and not speech. It follows verbs conjugated in ない form (with ない removed).

いられます is the potential form of いる.

Here again we have ても paired with a wh-word (in this case どんな), which takes on the meaning "no matter (what kind of)…" Thus the phrase どんなことがあっても means, "no matter what (kind of thing) happens."

A verb conjugated with the ending 〜てはいけません, means "don't do (verb)" or "you must not do (verb)". Note that this is slightly different from the grammar we saw earlier with 帰らなくてはいけません, because here 開ける is not in negative form. So in this case, the literal translation is, "If you open it, it's no good."

「それでは私の背中に乗ってください」と、亀が出てき
て言いました。
　浦島太郎は玉手箱を抱えて亀の背中に乗って、あっとい
う間に故郷の浜に着きました。
　しかし，何とかそこは以前の村とは違っているように思
えました。周辺を歩いてみたのですが、誰も知っている者が
いないのです。慌てて自分の家の方へ駆けていきました。し
かし、自分の家があった辺りには草が生えていて、家もなく、
母の姿も見えません。

それでは　　Well then
抱える【かかえる】To carry under or in arms
故郷【こきょう】Home town
何とか【なんとか】Somehow, something or other
以前【いぜん】Before
村【むら】Village
違う【ちがう】To differ (from)
ように　　Like
思える【おもえる】To seem
周辺【しゅうへん】Vicinity, environs
歩く【あるく】To walk
誰【だれ】Who
慌てて【あわてて】In a rush
自分【じぶん】Oneself
の方へ【のほうへ】In the direction of
駆ける【かける】To run, dash
辺り【あたり】Vicinity
草【くさ】Grass
生える【はえる】To grow

When movement verbs (like 歩く, 行く, etc.) are paired with the を particle, this marks the "path" that the movement was done on. For example, 川を渡る 【わたる】 means, "to cross the river." So 周辺を歩く means, "to walk in the vicinity" and not *"to walk to the vicinity."

There are a number of words in Japanese that take the も particle and pair it with a negative verb like 誰 does here. We saw in The Cat's Teacup that when 何 is followed by も and a negative verb, it takes on the meaning, "nothing." This is a characteristic of many other wh-words, among them 誰, "who," which takes on the meaning, "nobody." 誰も without the negative means, "everyone," it is only when it is followed by a negative verb that it takes on the meaning, "no one." A similar pairing occurs in the next section.

「わたしの家は、どうなったのだろう？　みんなはどこかへ、引っ越したのだろうか？」

でも、出会った人に尋ねても誰も家のことを知らないのです。浦島太郎はすっかり変わってしまった村のあちこちを歩き回りました。でも、知っている人は一人もいなく、家のことや母のことを尋ねても首を傾げるばかりです。

みんな　Everyone
どこか　Somewhere
引っ越す【ひっこす】To move (residence)
出会う【であう】To meet (by chance)
尋ねる【たずねる】To ask, inquire
すっかり　Completely
変わる【かわる】To change
あちこち　Here and there
歩き回る【あるきまわる】To walk around
一人【ひとり】One person
傾げる【かしげる】To tilt, lean
ばかり　Just, only

In the last sentence we see 一人もいない. If you remember from The Cat's Teacup, the も particle following 一人 is used with a meaning like "as much as." It is the opposite of using しか（＋ない）. However, here も is followed by a negative, so 一人もいない means "not so much as a single person." We will see another instance of も being used this way a little later.

「あの、すみません。浦島の家を知りませんか？」

浦島太郎が一人の老人に尋ねてみると、老人は少し首を傾げて言いました。

「浦島？　・・・ああ、たしか浦島という人なら三百年ほど前に海へ出たまま帰らないそうですよ」

「えっ！？」

老人の話しを聞いて、浦島太郎はびっくり。

老人【ろうじん】Old person
少し【すこし】A little
たしか　If I remember correctly
ほど　Approximately
そう　I hear that…
えっ！　What!

When なら follows a noun instead of the expected particle, it means that the following part of the sentence applies only to that noun. It can be used to emphasize the topic as it does here. For example, コンビニならあそこにありますよ is like saying, "If it's a convenience store you're looking for, it's over there." But this use of なら doesn't always translate well.

The final sentence here ends without a verb, perhaps to give it a little more punch to mirror the shock of the character. In proper form it would end with びっくりしました.

　わずか一年ほど竜宮で暮らしたと思っていたのに、本当は三百年も経っていたのです。竜宮の一年は、この世の三百年にあたるのでしょうか？

　（そんなばかな。）

　「家族も友だちも、みんな死んでしまったのか・・・」

　浦島太郎は玉手箱を抱えて、海辺へ戻ってきました。昔と変わらないのは海の景色だけです。どうすればいいかわからなくなりました。がっくりと肩を落とした浦島太郎は、ふと、持っていた玉手箱を見つめました。

わずか　　Merely, only

のに　　Despite, even though

本当【ほんとう】Truth

世【よ】World

にあたる　　Corresponds to

のでしょうか　　I wonder…

ばか　　Ridiculous, idiotic

家族【かぞく】Family

友だち【ともだち】Friends

死ぬ【しぬ】To die

昔【むかし】The past, a long time ago

景色【けしき】Scenery, landscape

どうすればいい　　What should I do?

がっくり　　Despondently

肩【かた】Shoulders

落とす【おとす】To lower, drop

Here is the other instance of where も is used with a meaning like "as much as."

「そう言えば、乙姫様は言っていたな。この玉手箱を開けると、『時』が戻ってしまうって。もしかしてこれを開けると、自分が暮らしていた時に戻る・・・」

　そう思った浦島太郎は、開けてはいけないと言われていた玉手箱を開けてしまいました。

　すると中から、真っ白の煙は出てきました。

　煙の中に、竜宮や美しい乙姫様の姿が映りました。そして楽しかった竜宮での一年が、次から次へと映し出されます。浦島太郎は、喜びました。

　でも玉手箱から出てきた煙は次第に薄れていき、その場に残ったのは髪もひげも真っ白になり、腰も曲がったおじいさんになった浦島太郎だったのです。

そう言えば【そういえば】That reminds me

もしかして　Perhaps

真っ白【まっしろ】Pure white

煙【けむり】Smoke

映る【うつる】To be projected

楽しい【たのしい】Fun, enjoyable

映し出す【うつしだす】To project

次第に【しだいに】Gradually

薄れる【うすれる】To fade, become dim

場【ば】Place, spot

残る【のこる】To remain

髪【かみ】Hair (on head)

ひげ　Beard

腰【こし】Back, waist

曲がる【まがる】To bend, curve

In the first sentence, って is used to quote what Lady Otohime said. It is equivalent to the と particle and verbs like 言う, 聞く, etc are normally dropped. It is only used in casual conversation (or in thoughts as it is here).

二月の桜

　昔々、桜谷というところに、おじいさんが孫と一緒に住んでいました。この桜谷には、昔から大きな桜の木があります。おじいさんは子供の頃から桜の木と友達で、春が来て満開の花を咲かせると、おじいさんは畑仕事もしないで桜をうっとりと眺めていました。そして花びらが散ると、おじいさんはその花びらを一枚一枚集めて木の下に埋めました。
　「桜は今年も楽しませてくれて、ありがとうよ」
　さて、そのおじいさんもやがて年を取り、とうとう動けなくなりました。

　二月のある寒い日、おじいさんは北風の音を聞きながら、ぽつんと若者に言いました。
　「わしは今まで生きてきて、本当に幸せだった。だが、死ぬ前にもう一度、あの桜の花を見たいものだ」
　「そんなことを言ったって、今は二月だ。いくらなんでも．．．」
　若者はそう言い掛けて、口をつぐみました。
　おじいさんが目を閉じて、涙をこぼしているのです。
　きっと、桜の花の姿を思い浮かべているのでしょう。
　「おじいさん、待って」
　若者はじっとしていられずに、外へ飛び出しました。そして冷たい北風の中を走って、桜の木の下に行きました。

　今日は特別に寒い日で、桜の木も凍えるように細い枝先を震わせています。若者は桜に手を合わせると、頼みました。

　「桜の木よ。どうか、お願いです。花を咲かせてください。おじいさんが死にそうなんです。おじいさんが生きている間に、もう一度花を見せてやりたいんです」
　若者は何度も祈り続けて、夜が来ても木の下を動こうとはしませんでした。

　やがて夜が明けて、朝が来ました。
　桜の木の下で祈り続けていた若者は、あまりの寒さで気を失っていましたが、急に暖かさを感じて目を覚ましました。

　「どうして、こんなに暖かいんだ？それに、甘い花の香りがするぞ」
　若者はゆっくりと顔を上げて、桜の木を見上げました。
　「あっ！」
　不思議なことに、桜の木には枝いっぱいに花が咲いていたのです。二月のこんなに寒い日に、しかもたった一晩で咲いたのです。
　「ありがとうございます！」
　若者は桜の木に礼を言うと、おじいさんの待つ家へ走って帰りました。

　「おじいさん！おじいさん！私がおんぶするから、一緒に来てください」
　「なんだ？どうしたんだ？」
　「いいから、出かけますよ」
　若者はおじいさんを背負うと、桜谷へと向かいました。やがて桜の木がだんだん近づいてくると、
　「おお...！」
　おじいさんは驚いて言葉も出せずに、ただ涙をぽろぽろとこぼしました。
　「よかったですね。おじいさん」
　桜の花は朝日を浴びて、キラキラと光り輝いています。

　「これほど見事な桜の花をわしは今まで見たことがない。わしは、本当に幸せ者だ」

　そうつぶやくおじいさんに、若者も涙をこぼしながら頷きました。

　それから間もなく、おじいさんは亡くなりましたが、それからも桜谷のこの桜の木は、毎年二月十六日になると見事な花を咲かせたそうです。

THE CHERRY TREE OF FEBRUARY

Once upon a time, an old man lived with his grandson in a place called Sakuradani. For many years there has been a large cherry blossom tree in Sakuradani. From the time he was a child, he was friends with the tree and when the cherry tree came into full bloom in Spring, the old man would stare raptly without doing so much as a stitch of work in the field. And, when the petals fell, the old man would gather them up one by one and bury them under the tree.

"Thank you for letting me enjoy you again this year, cherry tree."

Now, the old man soon became old too, until finally he could not move.

One cold day in February, the old man sighed while listening to the North Wind and said to the young man.

"All my life, I have lived really happily. But before I die, I would really like to see the flowers of that cherry blossom once more."

"That's easier said than done, it's February now! No matter how much..."

The young man started to say, then shut his mouth. Because the old man had his eyes closed and tears ran down his face. The image of the cherry blossom's flowers must have come to his mind.

"Grandfather, wait!"

Unable to keep still, the young man dashed outside and ran through the frigid North Wind to the base of the cherry tree.

On that day it was particularly cold and the thin branches shook as though the cherry blossom tree also was freezing. The young man clasped his hands and begged of the tree.

"Cherry tree. Please, I'm begging you. Please make your flowers bloom. Because my grandfather is on his death-bed and I would like you to show your flowers once more while he lives."

The young man implored over and over endlessly and even though night came, he did not try to move from beneath the tree.

Eventually, day dawned and morning came.

The young man, who had continued to plead beneath the cherry blossom tree, had lost consciousness from the extreme cold, but suddenly felt a warmth and opened his eyes.

"Why is it this warm? And I smell the sweet fragrance of flowers."

The young man slowly raised his face and looked at the cherry tree.

"Oh!"

Strangely enough, each and every branch in the cherry blossom tree had bloomed. All on such a cold day in February, and what's more, all in just one night.

"Thank you!"

The young man thanked the cherry tree then ran back to the house where the old man waited.

"Grandfather! Grandfather! Please come with me—I'll carry you on my back."

"What? What happened?"

"Come on, we're going out."

The young man took his grandfather on his back and headed for Sakuradani. Soon, the cherry tree came closer and closer and—

"Ah!"

The old man simply cried in astonishment, raining large tears, without being able to utter so much as a word.

"Isn't it great, grandfather?"

The cherry blossoms were bathed in morning light, glittering and sparkling.

"Never in my life have I seen such magnificent flowers as this. I am one lucky man."

When his grandfather uttered these words, the young man nodded in agreement as tears streamed forth.

Soon after that, the old man passed away, but ever since then it is said that the cherry tree of Sakuradani blooms with magnificent flowers every year on February 16th.

VOCABULARY AND GLOSS

　昔々、桜谷というところに、おじいさんが孫と一緒に住んでいました。この桜谷には、昔から大きな桜の木があります。おじいさんは子供の頃から桜の木と友達で、春が来て満開の花を咲かせると、おじいさんは畑仕事もしないで桜をうっとりと眺めていました。そして花びらが散ると、おじいさんはその花びらを一枚一枚集めて木の下に埋めました。

桜谷【さくらだに】Sakuradani
孫【まご】Grandchild
昔から【むかしから】From way back (the past)
桜の木【さくらのき】Cherry blossom tree
頃【ころ】Approximate time
春【はる】Spring
満開【まんかい】Full bloom
花【はな】Flower
咲かせる【さかせる】To make bloom
畑【はたけ】Field (farming)
畑仕事【はたしごと】Working in the fields
うっとりと　Raptly, absorbedly
眺める【ながめる】To gaze at
花びら【はなびら】Petal (flower)
散る【ちる】To fall (blossoms, leaves)

一枚【いちまい】One thin flat object
集める【あつめる】To gather, collect
埋める【うめる】To bury

A few adjectives like 大きい, 小さい, and やわらかい can have their final い replaced with な instead (the meaning remains the same). However, this is only used to modify nouns, it is not used when the adjective stands alone. For example, *この木は大きだ is not said.

The 咲かせる used here is technically not causative form, because it can be conjugated as 咲かせさせる, but it has the same meaning and the same spelling as the causative form of 咲く. It is one of those idiosyncrasies of language and, honestly, is probably a distinction that only linguists need to worry about. In the next section, we will have our first true instance of causative form.

The difference between 子供の頃 and 子供の時 is that 頃 can express a range of time, whereas 時 refers to a particular instance. In most cases they are interchangeable, but if you aren't indicating exactly when something happened during your childhood, 子供の頃 sounds more natural.

In the second to last sentence, we encounter the phrase 畑仕事もしないで, which contains the verb phrase 畑仕事をする. Replacing を with も here makes the statement more emphatic, meaning something like, "so much as..." And conjugating する as しないで makes it mean, "without doing." Thus 畑仕事もしないで was translated as, "without doing so much as a stitch of work in the field."

「桜は今年も楽しませてくれて、ありがとうよ」
　さて、そのおじいさんもやがて年を取り、とうとう動け
なくなりました。

　二月のある寒い日、おじいさんは北風の音を聞きながら、
ぽつんと若者に言いました。
　「わしは今まで生きてきて、本当に幸せだった。だが、
死ぬ前にもう一度、あの桜の花を見たいものだ」

今年【ことし】This year
楽しむ【たのしむ】To enjoy (oneself)
さて　　Well, now, then
やがて　　Soon, before long
年を取る【としをとる】To grow old
とうとう　　Finally, at last
動く【うごく】To move
北風【きたかぜ】North wind
音【おと】Sound
聞こえる【きこえる】Is heard, audible
ぽつんと　　Sighing while saying
若者【わかもの】Young person
わし　　I (older male)
今まで【いままで】Until now
生きる【いきる】To live
幸せ【しあわせ】Happiness
死ぬ【しぬ】To die
もう一度【もういちど】Once more, again

Here is the first true instance of causative form. Causative
form gives the verb either the meaning, "make" or "let" depending
on context. Since the verb here is 楽しむ, "to enjoy (oneself),"
clearly the meaning is let. This grammar can be a little
complicated, because we have to figure out who is letting the verb

happen (the director) and who is carrying it out (the actor). Particles make this simple: は marks the director and に marks the actor. However, more often than not one or both are left out of the sentence as they are here. This sentence could be written more explicitly as 桜はわしに楽しませてくれて、ありがとう but the てくれる conjugation makes it obvious that the old man is the actor, so わしに would be redundant.

When verbs are conjugated in short form, they have the same meaning as て-form; however, this is only used in writing, not speech.

The word もの is used at the end of sentences with various meanings, so it is sometimes difficult to determine which meaning is being employed, but here it is being used to express emotional involvement. This makes the 〜たいものだ conjugation stronger than just 〜たい (which means, "want to (verb)" as we saw in the last book).

「そんなことを言ったって、今は二月だ。いくらなんでも．．．」
　若者はそう言い掛けて、口をつぐみました。
　おじいさんが目を閉じて、涙をこぼしているのです。
　きっと、桜の花の姿を思い浮かべているのでしょう。

いくらなんでも　　Under no circumstances, there is no way
言い掛ける【いいかける】To start to say
口【くち】をつぐむ　　To hold one's tongue
目【め】Eyes
閉じる【とじる】To close
涙【なみだ】Tears
こぼす　　To shed (tears)
きっと　　Almost certainly
姿【すがた】Image, shape
思い浮かべる【おもいうかべる】Is reminded of

The phrase そんなことを言ったって is a phrase meaning something like, "that's easier said than done" or "that's easy for you to say." Phrases like this can be a little frustrating because it's hard to tell whether って is a conjugation, abbreviation, or particle. Here it is being used to mean, "even if," so a more literal translation of the phrase is, "even if (you) say such a thing."

掛ける is another auxiliary verb that adds the meaning, "begin but not complete."

When the copula is changed to でしょう or だろう, uncertainty is added. It corresponds to adding "probably" to a sentence. This is often paired with words like きっと or たぶん, but きっと makes the phrase a little more certain than just でしょう. きっと is used for about 90% certainty.

「おじいさん、待って」

若者はじっとしていられずに、外へ飛び出しました。そして冷たい北風の中を走って、桜の木の下に行きました。

今日は特別に寒い日で、桜の木も凍えるように細い枝先を震わせています。若者は桜に手を合わせると、頼みました。

「桜の木よ。どうか、お願いです。花を咲かせてください。おじいさんが死にそうなんです。おじいさんが生きている間に、もう一度花を見せてやりたいんです」

若者は何度も祈り続けて、夜が来ても木の下を動こうとはしませんでした。

じっと　Motionlessly
外【そと】Outside
飛び出す【とびだす】To rush, dash
冷たい【つめたい】Chilly, cold
走る【はしる】To run
特別に【とくべつに】Particularly
凍える【こごえる】To freeze
細い【ほそい】Thin
枝先【えださき】Tip of branch
震う【ふるう】To tremble, shake
合わせる【あわせる】To join together
頼む【たのむ】To beg, request
どうか　Please
お願い【おねがい】A wish, request
見せる【みせる】To show, display
何度も【なんども】Many times over
祈る【いのる】To wish for
続ける【つづける】To continue
夜【よる】Night, evening

The phrase じっとして いられずに might seem daunting at first, but is easily broken down. The adverb じっと is often used with 見る and 見つめる to mean, "look fixedly," or "stare," but when している is directly attached to it, it means, "to keep still." And if we remember back to 雪女, where we encountered the phrase, にもかかわらず, we know that the ending ず is the classical form of なくて and carries the same meaning. Also note that いる is in potential form, so the whole phrase means, "without being able to keep still." We will see another similar construction at the very end of the story.

続ける is an auxiliary verb that adds the meaning, "continue doing…"

In the story, The Child-rearing Ghost, we saw that the volitional form of a verb followed by とする gives the meaning, "make an effort to do (verb)." Here, we have 動こうとはしませんでした. The は is added because of the negative. The は doesn't change the meaning, but for some reason Japanese people like to have a は in negative sentences.

やがて夜が明けて、朝が来ました。
　桜の木の下で祈り続けていた若者は、あまりの寒さで気
を失っていましたが、急に暖かさを感じて目を覚ましました。

　「どうして、こんなに暖かいんだ？それに、甘い花の香
りがするぞ」
　若者はゆっくりと顔を上げて、桜の木を見上げました。
　「あっ！」
　不思議なことに、桜の木には枝いっぱいに花が咲いてい
たのです。二月のこんなに寒い日に、しかもたった一晩で咲
いたのです。

明ける【あける】To grow bright, dawn
朝【あさ】Morning
あまりの　Such
気を失う【きをうしなう】To lose consciousness
急に【きゅうに】Suddenly
暖かい【あたたかい】Warm
感じる【かんじる】To feel
目を覚ます【めをさます】
どうして　Why?
こんなに　Like this, so
それに　And, moreover
甘い【あまい】Sweet
香り【かおり】Fragrance, aroma
ゆっくりと Slowly
顔【かお】Face
上げる【あげる】To raise, lift
見上げる【みあげる】To look up at
不思議【ふしぎ】Strange, mysterious
枝【えだ】Branch
いっぱい　Full, at capacity
しかも　Besides that, moreover
たった　Only, merely

一晩【いちばん】 One evening, night

The way to say that something smells good, bad, etc is a little different in Japanese than in English. In Japanese, the verb する is used; for example, これはいいにおいがする corresponds to, "This smells good," in English even though it looks like it means, "This makes a good smell." Likewise with 香り, saying これは甘い香りがする means, "This smells sweet."

We can use adjectives to make a transitional adverb by pairing them with ことに. In the story, 不思議 is paired in this way, to make 不思議なことに, which means, "Strangely, …" or "Mysteriously, …" Another common example is 面白いことに, meaning, "Interestingly, …"   These are used at the beginning of sentences to transition from one thought to another or to transition to a new subject.

The ending さ can be added to adjectives to turn them into a noun. For い-adjectives, さ replaces い and for な-adjectives it replaces な.

「ありがとうございます！」
　若者は桜の木に礼を言うと、おじいさんの待つ家へ走って帰りました。

　「おじいさん！おじいさん！私がおんぶするから、一緒に来てください」
　「なんだ？どうしたんだ？」
　「いいから、出かけますよ」
　若者はおじいさんを背負うと、桜谷へと向かいました。やがて桜の木がだんだん近づいてくると、
　「おお...！」

礼【れい】Thanks
待つ【まつ】To wait
家【いえ】House, home
おんぶする
一緒に【いっしょに】Together
どうしたんだ　What happened?
いいから　Come on, listen up
出かける【でかける】To go out, depart
背負う【せおう】
向かう【むかう】
だんだん
近づく【ちかづく】

　いいから　is used at the beginning of a sentence in which a command is issued and literally means, "because it's good." It is used to provide emphasis to the command, to try to cajole another person into doing something. However, there is no English equivalent, so it can be difficult to translate.

おじいさんは驚いて言葉も出せずに、ただ涙をぽろぽろ
とこぼしました。
　「よかったですね。おじいさん」
　桜の花は朝日を浴びて、キラキラと光り輝いています。
　「これほど見事な桜の花をわしは今まで見たことがない。
わしは、本当に幸せ者だ」
　そうつぶやくおじいさんに、若者も涙をこぼしながら頷
きました。

　それから間もなく、おじいさんは亡くなりましたが、そ
れからも桜谷のこの桜の木は、毎年二月十六日になると見事
な花を咲かせたそうです。

驚く【おどろく】Is surprised, astonished
言葉【ことぼ】Word
出す【だす】To produce (a sound)
ただ　Only, just
ぽろぽろ　In large drops
朝日【あさひ】Morning sun
浴びる【あびる】To bask in, be flooded with
キラキラ　Sparkle, twinkle
光り輝く【ひかりかがやく】To glitter
これほど　This much
見事な【みごとな】Magnificent, splendid
幸せ者【しあわせもの】Fortunate person
つぶやく　To murmur
頷く【うなずく】To nod
それから　And then, after that
間もなく【まもなく】Soon, before long
亡くなる【なくなる】To pass away
そう　It is said that…, I hear…

The phrase 言葉も出せずに is packed with grammar we've
learned. As we saw at the beginning of the story, the も here

makes the statement more emphatic, meaning something like, "so much as a..." And the combination of potential from and ず gives the phrase the meaning, "without being able to utter so much as a word." (It's a little amazing that the Japanese language can pack so much into such a short statement. ^ ^)

The そう at the very end of the story does not mean, "seems," but is used to report hearsay. It has the same meaning as ということだ.

一寸法師

　昔々、あるところに仲のいい夫婦がいました。二人には子供がいなかったので、毎日お宮へ出かけて、ぽんぽんと手を打って、「どうかわしらに子供をくれてください。親指くらいの小さな子供でも結構ですから」と、お願いしていました。
　するとある日、驚いたことに、小さな赤ちゃんが生まれました。本当に親指くらいの男の子です。
　「おう、おう。かわいいね。生まれたばかりで、今はこんなに小さいが、そのうち大きな元気な子になるだろう」
　二人はさっそく、その子に一寸法師という名前を付けてやって、大事に育てることにしました。年を取った夫婦は大喜びです。

　一寸法師は元気に育ってきました。けれども、背が少しも大きくなりません。

　ある日のこと、一寸法師は夫婦に、畳に手をついて、こう言いました。
　「お父さん、お母さん、これから私は首都へ行って働きたいと思います。立派な武士になって、戻ってきます」
　そこでお父さんは一本の針で、一寸法師にちょうどピッタリの大きさの刀を作ってやりました。お母さんは器と箸で、一寸法師の乗る舟を作ってやりました。
　「体に気をつけるんだよ」
　「危ないことはしないでね」
　「大丈夫です。それでは行ってきます」

　一寸法師はお父さんとお母さんに見送れて、さっそく首都へ向かいました。
　途中、アリに会い、
　「アリさん、川はどこですか」
　「タンポポ畑のところです」
　一寸法師は川に着くと、器に飛び乗り、矢のように川を下っていきました。途中で魚が彼を食べ物だと間違えて向かってきました。しかし、一寸法師は箸を使って魚を追い払いました。
　波に揺られ、雨に打たれ、風に吹かれ、何日もかかって、やっと首都に着きました。
　首都はにぎやかです。たくさんの人が、急いで歩いています。馬や馬車も通ります。
　「踏み潰されてしまう。用心。用心」
　一寸法師は周りに気をつけながら、道を歩いていきました。すると立派な門のある屋敷の前に出ました。そこで働くことを思いつきました。
　「ごめんください。お願いがあります」
　「はーい。・・・あれ？」
　出て来た手伝いの人は、首をかしげました。
　「おや、誰もいないねえ」
　と、立ち去っていきました。
　そこで、もう一度、
　「ごめんください！」
　お腹の底から、大声で呼びました。
　今度は屋敷の中から主人が出てきて、キョロキョロ辺りを見回しました。
　「はて。一体誰だ？誰も見えん。妙だな」
　「ここだよ！あなたの足元にいます」
　主人は靴の影に立っている、小さな一寸法師をやっと見つけました。
　「あれまあ、なんて小さい子だろう」
　主人は一寸法師を摘んで、手のひらに乗せました。
　「私は一寸法師と申します。どうかこのお屋敷で働かせてください。お願いいたします」
　一寸法師は丁寧に頭を下げました。
　「お前はなかなか活発で頭が良さそうだ。よし家来にしてやろう」

　主人は喜んで一寸法師の願いを聞き入れてくれました。
　そうして働くことになった屋敷には美しい娘がおり、一寸法師はその娘から読み書きを教わりました。一寸法師は頭が良くてすぐ理解してしまいました。やがて、一日中一緒に部屋の中で遊んでいて、娘は一寸法師が大好きになりました。

　ある日のこと、娘は一寸法師を連れてお寺にお参りに行きました。するとその帰り道、突然、森の中から二匹の鬼が飛び出して、娘をさらおうとしました。
　「何をするんだ？」
と、一寸法師は針の刀を抜いて、鬼に飛び掛かっていきました。
　「生意気な。食ってしまう」と、鬼は言うと、一寸法師を摘み上げて、一気に飲み込んでしまいました。
　鬼のお腹の中は真っ暗です。何も見えません。一寸法師は針の刀を振り回して、お腹の中を刺しながら走り回ったから、たまりません。
　「い、痛たた、痛たたたた．．．」
　鬼は苦しくなって転げ回り、慌てて一寸法師を吐き出しました。
　「お前が食わないなら、俺が食う」
　もう一匹の鬼が、一寸法師を摘んで、口に入れようとしました。でも、一寸法師は、するりと鬼の手から逃れると、刀で鬼の目に刺しました。
　「たっ、たっ、助けてくれー！これはたまらん！」
　二匹の鬼は泣きながら慌てて逃げ出しました。
　「もう二度と来るな！」
　「助けてくれてありがとう。あなたは小さくても、とても勇気で強いのね」　と娘は言いました。
　「見てください。鬼が何か忘れていきました。これは何でしょう」
　鬼が逃げていった後に、一寸法師は不思議な物が落ちていたことに気付きました。
　「まあ、これは魔法のワンドですよ。トントンと振りながら望みを言えば、何でも好きな物が出てくると言いますよ」
　そこで一寸法師は、娘に頼みました。
　「それなら、わたしの背が伸びるように『背出ろ、背出ろ』と、そう言って振ってください」

　娘は喜んで、ワンドを振りました。
　「背出ろ、背出ろ」
　すると、一寸法師の体がどんどん伸びて、立派な若者になりました。
　小さくてよくわかりませんでしたが、見れば見るほど美しい顔をしています。その上、恐ろしい鬼を倒すほど強い若者だ。
　それから、年を取ったお父さんとお母さんを首都に呼んで、一寸法師は娘と結婚しました。仕事もがんばり、望んだ通り立派な武士になりました。そして美しい娘と一緒に、いつまでも幸せに暮らしたそうです。

THE INCH-HIGH SAMURAI

Long ago in a certain place, there lived a very close husband and wife. Since the couple did not have any children, they went out to a shrine every day, clapped their hands together, and implored, "Please grant us a child. Even a tiny child the size of my thumb would be fine."

And one day, to their surprise, a tiny child was born. It really was the size of the man's thumb.

"Oh, oh. He's cute, isn't he! He's so small because he was just born, but before long, he'll surely become a large, healthy child."

The couple at once gave the child the name, Issunboushi, The Inch High Samurai, and agreed to raise him with great care. The old couple was overjoyed.

Issunboushi grew up healthy; however, his height didn't increase at all.

One day, Issunboushi prostrated himself before the husband and wife and spoke thus,

"Father, Mother, I think I'd like to go to the capital. I will become fine warrior and then return here."

So his father made him a katana from a pin that was exactly the right size for him. His mother made him a boat that he could ride on from a bowl and chopsticks.

"Take care of yourself."

"Don't do anything risky."

"I'll be okay. Well then, I'll be on my way."

Issunboushi was seen off by his father and mother and then headed off toward the capital at once.

On the way, he met an ant.

"Mr. Ant, where is the river?"

"It's in the dandelion field."

When Issunboushi arrived at the river, he leaped onto his bowl, and shot down the river like an arrow. On the way, a fish mistook him for food and came toward him, but Issunboushi used his chopsticks to drive the fish off.

He was rocked by waves, hammered by rain, tossed by the wind, until at last he reached the capital after many days.

The capital was bustling. Many people were walking hurriedly. Horses and carriages also passed by.

"I'm going to get trampled. Look out. Look out."

Keeping a watchful eye on everything around him, Issunboushi walked down the street. And then he came before a magnificent mansion with a gate. It occurred to him that he should work there.

"Hello? Is anyone home? I have a favor to ask."

"Coming!...Huh?"

The maid that came forth tilted her head to the side.

"Oh, there's no one here," she said and left.

So, once again, "Hello? Is anyone home?" he called with a loud voice, from deep in his belly.

This time the master of the house came from inside the mansion, and looked around the vicinity edgily.

"Well, who in the world is it? I don't see anyone. Most peculiar..."

"I'm here! I'm at your feet!"

At last, the master of the house noticed small Issunboushi standing in the shadow of his shoes.

"Oh my, what a small child!"

The master of the house picked Issunboushi up and set the boy in the palm of his hand.

"My name is Issunboushi. Please allow me to work in your home. I beseech you."

"You seem very active and smart. Alright, I'll make you my retainer."

The master of the house gladly granted Issunboushi's wish.

And, in the mansion where it was decided that he would work, there was a beautiful girl, and the girl taught Issunboushi reading and writing. Since Issunboushi was smart, understood at once. And before long, they were spending all day long together in her room, and the girl grew fond of Issunboushi.

One day, the girl took Issunboushi on a shrine visit. And on their way home, suddenly two ogres rushed out from the woods and tried to kidnap the girl.

"What are you doing!?" Issunboushi pulled out his needle katana and threw himself at the ogres.

"Cheeky, aren't you? I'm gonna eat you," the ogre said then picked Issunboushi up and swallowed him up in one gulp.

Inside the ogre's stomach it was pitch black. Nothing was visible. Issunboushi waved his needle katana around and ran around, stabbing inside the stomach, making it unbearable for the ogre.

"Ow, oww, ooowwwwwww!!"

The ogre rolled around in pain and hastily spat Issunboushi out.

"If you're not going to eat him, I'll eat him."

The other ogre picked Issunboushi up and tried to put him in its mouth. But Issunboushi slipped out from the ogre's hand and stabbed it in the eye with his katana.

"He…he…heeelp! This is unbearable!"

The two ogres hastily ran away crying.

"Don't come back again!"

"Thank you for saving me. Even though you are small, you are very brave and strong aren't you," the young girl said.

"Look here. The ogres left something behind. What is this, do you think?"

After the ogres ran away, Issunboushi noticed they had dropped a strange object.

"It would seem this is a magic wand. It is said that if you make a wish while waving it, you can make anything you like appear."

So Issunboushi asked the girl, "In that case, will you please wave the wand and say, 'Height come forth, height come forth,' so that my height will grow?"

The girl waved the wand with joy, "Height come forth, height come forth."

And then Issunboushi's body grew rapidly and he turned into a handsome young man.

Since he was small, it wasn't readily apparent, but the more one looks, the more beautiful a face he has. On top of that, he was a young man who was strong enough to defeat terrifying ogres.

After that, he invited his aged father and mother to the capital and married the girl. He worked hard and became a fine warrior just like he wished. And it's said that, together with the beautiful girl, he lived happily until the end of time.

VOCABULARY AND GLOSS

　昔々、あるところに仲のいい夫婦がいました。二人には子供がいなかったので、毎日お宮へ出かけて、ぽんぽんと手を打って、「どうかわしらに子供をくれてください。親指くらいの小さな子供でもけっこうですから」と、お願いしていました。
　するとある日、驚いたことに、小さな赤ちゃんが生まれました。本当に親指くらいの男の子です。

仲【なか】Relationship
仲のいい　Close, intimate
夫婦【ふうふ】Couple, spouses
子供【こども】Children
毎日【まいにち】Everyday
お宮【おみや】Shinto Shrine
出かける【でかける】To go out, set out
ぽんぽんと Bang-bang, tap-tap
手を打つ【てをうつ】To clap hands
どうか　Please
親指【おやゆび】Thumb
くらい　Approximately
けっこう　Fine, okay
お願い【おねがい】Request, wish
赤ちゃん【あかちゃん】Baby
生まれる【うまれる】Is born

When saying things like "I have two brothers," or "She has three kids," the particle に is attached to the noun that has them. For example, to say, "I have an older sister," you can say, 私には姉がいる.

Attaching the particle でも to a noun makes the noun less definite. It's like saying, "or something" or "even." So, when the couple says, 親指くらいの小さな子供でもけっこう, they are not saying they want a child that is about the size of their thumb, they're saying even something like that would suffice.

We saw in the last story that adjectives can be combined with ことに to make an adverb and here we see this can also be done with certain verbs: 驚いたことに. Unsurprisingly, this means "surprisingly" or "to (my) surprise."

「おう、おう。かわいいね。生まれたばかりで、今はこんなに小さいが、そのうち大きな元気な子になるだろう」
　二人はさっそく、その子に一寸法師という名前を付けてやって、大事に育てることにしました。年を取った夫婦は大喜びです。

　一寸法師は元気に育ってきました。けれども、背が少しも大きくなりません。

そのうち　　Eventually, before long
さっそく　　At once, without delay
一寸法師【いっすんぼうし】The inch high samurai
名前【なまえ】Name
付ける【つける】To attach
大事【だいじ】Important, valuable
育てる【そだてる】To bring up, rear
年を取る【としをとる】To grow old
大喜び【おおよろこび】Great joy
育つ【そだつ】To grow up, be raised
けれども　　But
背【せ】Height, stature
少しも【すこしも】*See below

When a verb is in past tense and is followed by ばかり, this makes it mean, "just did (verb)." For example, 今帰ったばかりだ。 means, "I just returned now." So, in the story, 生まれたばかり means, "(He) was just born." (The で following ばかり is just the て-form of だ/です.)

Adjectives are sometimes stacked together like 大きな元気な子, especially in speech. It has the obvious meaning of, "Big, energetic child."

It should be pretty obvious that 大 is a prefix that adds the meaning, "great" or "big" etc. The only problem is that it is sometimes pronounced おお and sometimes だい. For example, 大口【おおぐち】 means, "a big mouth" (as in someone who boasts a lot); and 大問題【だいもんだい】 means, "a big problem." We will see this prefix again in a bit.

けれども is the formal version of けど.

When 少しも is combined with a negative form, it takes on the meaning, "not one bit." For example, フランス語を少しも知らない means, "I don't know any French."

　ある日のこと、一寸法師は夫婦に、畳に手をついて、こう言いました。

　「お父さん、お母さん、これから私は首都へ行って働きたいと思います。立派な武士になって、戻ってきます」

　そこでお父さんは一本の針で、一寸法師にちょうどピッタリの大きさの刀を作ってやりました。お母さんは器と箸で、一寸法師の乗る舟を作ってやりました。

畳【たたみ】 Tatami mats
手をつく To place both hands on ground
首都【しゅと】 Capital City
働く【はたらく】 To work, labor
立派【りっぱ】 Splendid, fine
武士【ぶし】 Warrior, samurai

戻る【もどる】To return, go back
そこで　So, accordingly
一本【いっぽん】One long cylindrical thing
針【はり】Needle, pin
ちょうど　Exactly
ピッタリ　Precisely
刀【かたな】Katana, sword
作る【つくる】To make
器【うつわ】Bowl
箸【はし】Chopsticks
乗る【のる】To ride
船【ふね】Boat

Old stories like this one use 都, but since this word is no longer commonly used, it has been replaced with 首都, which you will hear and read.

The difference between using 〜たいと思う and just plain 〜たい is that the former is more objective.

The の in 一寸法師の乗る has replaced が. This is often done to reduce the number of は's and が's in a sentence, as long sentences can contain quite a few. This is done either to make the subject or topic more apparent or just to make the sentence sound less repetitive and doesn't change the meaning. Sometimes, though, it is used to give the subject of the clause and the noun that the clause modifies a slightly closer bond (in this case 一寸法師 and 舟) although the difference is subtle and may not be picked up by everyone.

Cultural Note:

If you have watched any samurai movies or period dramas 時代劇【じだいげき】, you have probably seen the act of 手を突く【つく】. It's when an inferior kneels before their lord and bows their head, placing both hands on the ground, in order to present a request, apologize, or to express respect. However, it can also just mean placing your hands on the table or ground in a more general sense.

「体に気をつけるんだよ」
「危ないことはしないでね」
「大丈夫です。それでは行ってきます」
　一寸法師はお父さんとお母さんに見送られて、さっそく首都へ向かいました。
　途中、一寸法師はアリに会い、
「アリさん、川はどこですか」
「タンポポ畑のところです」
　一寸法師は川に着くと、器に飛び乗り、矢のように川を下っていきました。途中で魚が一寸法師を食べ物だと間違えて向かってきました。しかし、一寸法師は箸を使って魚を追い払いました。

体【からだ】Body
気をつける　Take care, pay attention
危ない【あぶない】Dangerous
大丈夫【だいじょうぶ】Okay
それでは　Well then
見送る【みおくる】To see off
向かう【むかう】To head toward
途中【とちゅう】On the way
アリ　Ant
会う【あう】To meet
タンポポ畑【はた】Dandelion field
着く【つく】To arrive at, reach
飛び乗る【とびのる】To jump upon
矢【や】Arrow
下る【くだる】To go down
魚【さかな】Fish
食べ物【たべもの】Food
間違える【まちがえる】To confuse, make a mistake
使う【つかう】To use
追い払う【おいはらう】To drive away

We encountered 見送る previously in Kasajizou, but since it is in passive form here, it is easier to tell who was being seen off.

When using the verb 会う, the person being met takes the に particle. For example, 友達に会った。 means, "I met a friend." And with the verb 着く, the destination takes the に particle. For example, 彼はホテルに着いた。 means, "He arrived at the hotel."

The compound verb 飛び乗る literally means, "jump and ride," so it is usually used for jumping onto moving objects like a train. However, it can also be used for non-moving objects like jumping onto a table or chair.

Cultural Note

Hopefully you've seen and heard 行ってきます; this is what people in Japan say when leaving the house for school, work, or whatever. It literally means, "I'll go and come back." Whomever is home and is not leaving responds, 行ってらっしゃい. らっしゃい is a shortened imperative form of いらっしゃる, which, if you know your keigo, is the honorific form of 来る/行く. So, the same thing is being said in response, only in honorific imperative form.

　波に揺られ、雨に打たれ、風に吹かれ、何日もかかって、や
っと首都に着きました。
　首都はにぎやかです。たくさんの人が、急いで歩いています。
馬や馬車も通ります。
　「踏み潰されてしまう。用心。用心」
　一寸法師は周りに気をつけながら、道を歩いていきました。
すると立派な門のある屋敷の前に出ました。一寸法師はそこで働
くことを思いつきました。

波【なみ】Waves
揺る【ゆる】To rock, swing
打つ【うつ】To strike, hit
吹く【ふく】To blow (wind)
何日も【なんにちも】For several days
かかる　To take (time)
やっと　At last; barely
にぎやか　Lively, busy
馬【うま】Horse
馬車【ばしゃ】Carriage
通る【とおる】To go past
踏み潰す【ふみつぶす】To trample
用心【ようじん】Look out
周り【まわり】Surroundings
道【みち】Road
すると　Whereupon, and then
門【もん】Gate
屋敷【やしき】Mansion
出る【でる】To appear, come forth
思いつく【おもいつく】To think of, be struck by an idea

The verbs 揺る and 震える【ふるえる】both mean shake, but 揺
る describes a rocking motion like that of waves, a cradle, etc. And as
we saw in The Snow Woman, 震える is used for trembling motions like
shivering.

「ごめんください。お願いがあります」
「はーい。・・・あれ？」
出て来た手伝いの人は、首をかしげました。
「おや、誰もいないねえ」
と、立ち去っていきました。
そこで、もう一度、
「ごめんください！」
お腹の底から、大声で呼びました。

あれ？　Eh?
手伝い【てつだい】Helper
首【くび】Neck, head
かしげる　To tilt, lean
おや　Oh
誰も【だれも】*See below
立ち去る【たちさる】To leave
もう一度【いちぢ】Once more
お腹【おなか】Stomach
底【そこ】Bottom
大声【おおごえ】Loud voice
呼ぶ【よぶ】To call

Cultural Note:
たのもう is what a samurai would say when he stops by a house, dojo, etc, but since this will almost never be heard or read, it was replaced with the modern equivalent, ごめんください. This is the equivalent to, "Hello? Is anybody home?" and is what Japanese people say when they knock on the door. (They also often just walk in the house and say this.) When someone is invited in to a home, they say, じゃまします, which is similar to, "Sorry to intrude..."

　今度は屋敷の中から主人が出てきて、キョロキョロ辺りを見
回しました。
　「はて。一体誰だ？誰も見えん。妙だな」
　「ここだよ！あなたの足元にいます」
　主人は靴の影に立っている、小さな一寸法師をやっと見つけ
ました。
　「あれまあ、なんて小さい子だろう」
　主人は一寸法師を摘んで、手のひらに乗せました。

今度【こんど】This time
主人【しゅじん】Head of household
キョロキョロ　Looking around restlessly
辺り【あたり】Vicinity
見回す【みまわす】To look around
はて　Oh dear, well
一体【いったい】…in the world?
足元【あしもと】At one's feet
靴【くつ】Shoes
影【かげ】Shadow
立つ【たつ】To stand
見つける【みつける】To find, locate
あれまあ　Oh my gosh
摘む【つまむ】To pick up, pluck
手のひら【てのひら】Palm of the hand
乗せる【のせる】To place on (something)

We saw in The Child-Rearing Ghost that 一体 is an adverb that
makes questions more emphatic when it comes before an interrogative
word like 何 or 誰. Depending on how it is said and the context, 一体誰
can range from, "who in the world?" to the fiercer "who the hell?" and
beyond. There really are no swear words in Japanese; instead politeness
and inflection are used to express the same effect as swear words.

In casual speech, the negative ない can be shortened to just ん. So
the 主人 is saying 誰も見えない, "I don't see anyone" ("I see
nobody"). ない can also be changed to ねえ in casual speech. Both of
these forms are often used in anime and manga.

「私は一寸法師と申します。どうかこのお屋敷で働かせてください。お願いいたします」

一寸法師は丁寧に頭を下げました。

「お前はなかなか活発で頭が良さそうだ。よし家来にしてやろう」

主人は喜んで一寸法師の願いを聞き入れてくれました。

申す【もうす】To be called (Humb)
どうか　Please
お願いいたします Please
丁寧【ていねい】Polite
頭【あたま】Head
下げる【さげる】To lower, bow
お前【おまえ】You (informal)
なかなか　Very
活発【かっぱつ】Active, vigorous
頭が良い【あたまがいい】Intelligent
よし　Good
〜にする　To raise (someone) to a post
家来【けらい】Retainer, servant
喜ぶ【よろこぶ】To be pleased
聞き入れる【ききいれる】To grant (wish)

申す is the humble form of 言う and has the same meaning. 一寸法師 is speaking very respectfully to the 主人, which is why he adds the お to 屋敷 and uses お願いいたします, which is the honorific version of お願いします. (致す【いたす】is the humble form of する).

Notice that the 主人 speaks very casually to 一寸法師 and even uses てやる, which is less polite than てあげる. The 主人 also uses お前, which is not very polite to use with a stranger, but which is sometimes used between close friends.

The adjective いい is irregular and when adding そう to いい, the word is changed to よさそう instead of just replacing the final い with そう. This is easier to remember if you know that 良い can be pronounced either as いい or よい.

そうして働くことになった屋敷には美しい娘がおり、一寸法師はその娘から読み書きを教わりました。一寸法師は頭が良くてすぐ理解してしまいました。やがて、一日中一緒に部屋の中で遊んでいて、娘は一寸法師が大好きになりました。

　ある日のこと、娘は一寸法師を連れてお寺にお参りに行きました。するとその帰り道、突然、森の中から二匹の鬼が飛び出して、娘をさらおうとしました。

そうして　And
美しい【うつくしい】Beautiful
娘【むすめ】Young girl
おる　*See below
読み書き【よみかき】Reading and writing
教わる【おそわる】To be taught
すぐ　Immediately
理解【りかい】Understanding
一日中【いちにちじゅう】All day long
部屋【へや】Room
遊ぶ【あそぶ】To have a good time
大好き【だいすき】Like very much
連れる【つれる】To take (person)
お寺【おてら】Temple
お参り【おまいり】Shrine visit
帰り道【まえりみち】Return home
突然【とつぜん】Suddenly
森【もり】Forest
二匹【にひき】Two animals
鬼【おに】Ogre, demon
飛び出す【とびだす】To rush out, jump out
さらう　To abduct

The expression ことになる is similar to ことにする, but while ことにする describes a decision that the subject made, ことになる describes a decision that was made by someone or something else. Because of this, ことになる can sometimes be a little difficult to translate. It can take on several meanings from, "it has been decided/arranged that…" to "(I) ended up…" or even "it follows that…"

This is one of those parts of grammar, like は/が, that can't be mastered in one sitting.

If we remember from The Snow Woman, 娘 can mean one's own daughter, but it is also used to mean "girl."

It was mentioned before that when verbs are conjugated in short form, they have the same meaning as て-form; however, the short form of the verb いる, though, is just い, so it is changed to おり (which is the humble version of いる), when used in this way. So 娘がおり has the same meaning as 娘がいて, but has a more literary feel.

As noted above, the adjective いい is irregular, and when conjugated in て-form, it becomes よくて.

「何をするんだ？」
と、一寸法師は針の刀を抜いて、鬼に飛び掛かっていきました。
　「生意気な。食ってしまう」と、鬼は言うと、一寸法師を摘み上げて、一気に飲み込んでしまいました。
　鬼のお腹の中は真っ暗です。何も見えません。一寸法師は針の刀を振り回して、お腹の中を刺しながら走り回ったから、たまりません。
　「い、痛たた、痛たたたた．．．」
　鬼は苦しくなって転げ回り、慌てて一寸法師を吐き出しました。
　「お前が食わないなら、俺が食う」
　もう一匹の鬼が、一寸法師を摘んで、口に入れようとしました。でも、一寸法師は、するりと鬼の手から逃れると、刀で鬼の目に刺しました。

抜く【ぬく】To pull out, extract
飛び掛かる【とびかかる】To throw oneself upon
生意気【なまいき】Impertinent, cheeky
食う【くう】To eat (vulgar)
一気に【いっきに】In one go

飲み込む【のみこむ】To gulp down
真っ暗【まっくら】Total darkness
振り回す【ふりまわす】To wave around
刺す【さす】To stab
走り回る【はしりまわる】
たまらない　Unbearable
痛たた【いたた】Ouch
苦しい【くるしい】Painful, agonizing
転げ回る【ころげまわる】To roll around
慌てて【あわてて】In a rush
吐き出す【はきだす】To spit out, vomit
俺【おれ】I (rough)
もう一匹【もういっぴき】The other (animal)
入れる【いれる】To put in, insert
するりと　Smoothly, speedily
逃れる【のがれる】To escape
目【め】Eye

Note the use of が in お前が食わないなら、俺が食う．It's like saying, "If you are the one who isn't going to eat him, then I will be the one who eats him."　Basically, when we use が, we are answering the question *which?*　It's like pointing at something and saying, "this is the one."

「たっ、たっ、助けてくれー！これはたまらん！」
二匹の鬼は泣きながら慌てて逃げ出しました。
「もう二度と来るな！」
「助けてくれてありがとう。あなたは小さくても、とても勇
気で強いのね」　と娘は言いました。
「見てください。鬼が何か忘れていきました。これは何でし
ょう」

助ける【たすける】To help
泣く【なく】To cry
逃げ出す【にげだす】To run away
もう　Again
二度と【にどと】(+neg) Never again
勇気【ゆうき】Brave
強い【つよい】Strong
忘れる【わすれる】To forget

We saw a glimpse of imperative form in Taro Urashima and here we have two more small glimpses. The first is 助けてくれ, which is the imperative form of 助けてくれる. Basically, てくれ is a command to ask someone to do something for you. It's fine to use this form among friends, but if you're in a crowd of strangers or at work, it's better to yell, 助けて.

The second glimpse is a negative imperative. The conjugation of negative imperative is simple: just add な to the dictionary form of a verb. And this changes the sentence to a command not to do something. So when 一寸法師　says,　もう二度と来るな！, he is issuing the command, "Don't come again!" Also, 二度と is another one of those adverbs that is paired with a negative verb.

In the girls response, she says, あなたは小さくても. When a sentence is conjugated into て-form followed by も, this adds the meaning, "even though" or "even if." So あなたは小さくても means, "Even though you are small…" Another example is, これが好きでなくても、食べないといけないよ。meaning, "Even if you don't like this, you must eat it.

　鬼が逃げていった後に、一寸法師は不思議な物が落ちていた
ことに気付きました。
　「まあ、これは魔法のワンドですよ。トントンと振りながら
望みを言えば、何でも好きな物が出てくると言いますよ」
　そこで一寸法師は、娘に頼みました。
　「それなら、わたしの背が伸びるように『背出ろ、背出ろ』
と、そう言って振ってください」
　娘は喜んで、ワンドを振りました。
　「背出ろ、背出ろ」

逃げる 【にげる】 To escape, run away
不思議 【ふしぎ】 Strange, mysterious
物 【もの】 Object
落ちる 【おちる】 To fall, drop
気付く 【きづく】 To notice, become aware of
まあ　Well…, It would seem…
魔法 【まほう】 Magic
ワンド　Wand
トントン　Tap-tap
振る 【ふる】 To wave
望み 【のぞみ】 Wish, desire
何でも 【なんでも】 Whatever one likes
頼む 【たのむ】 To request, ask
それなら　If that's the case
伸びる 【のびる】 To extend, grow

When using 気付く, the に particle points to what was noticed. And
what was noticed must be in noun form, so if what was noticed is an
action, the verb needs to be nominalized with either の or こと as it is in:
一寸法師は不思議な物が落ちていたことに気付きました.

Just like in Taro Urashima, the ように following 背が伸びる does
not mean "like," it is used to express a desire or wish and so is usually
translated as "so that" or "in order to."

And here we have another use of imperative form. The conjugation
of 出る is irregular for imperative form: instead of changing to 出れ, it
becomes 出ろ.　So this incantation, 背出ろ, is a command for his
"height to come forth."

　すると、一寸法師の体がどんどん伸びて、立派な若者になりました。

　小さくてよくわかりませんでしたが、見れば見るほど美しい顔をしています。その上、恐ろしい鬼を倒すほど強い若者だ。

　それから、年を取ったお父さんとお母さんを首都に呼んで、一寸法師は娘と結婚しました。仕事もがんばり、望んだ通り立派な武士になりました。そして美しい娘と一緒に、いつまでも幸せに暮らしたそうです。

どんどん　　Rapidly
顔【かお】Face
その上【うえ】On top of that
恐ろしい【おそろしい】Frightening, terrifying
倒す【たおす】To defeat, knock down
呼ぶ【よぶ】To invite
結婚【けっこん】Marriage
仕事【しごと】Work
がんばる　　To do one's best
望む【のぞむ】To desire, wish for
〜通り【とおり】In accordance with
いつまでも　　Forever
幸せ【しあわせ】Happy
暮らす【くらす】To live, get along

The phrase 見れば見るほど might seem a little confusing at first because of the repeated 見る, but when a verb is conjugated into ば…ほど form, it gives the sentence the meaning, "the more…the more." However, the repeated verb isn't used twice in English, which is what makes this grammar a little confusing. For example, 聞けば聞くほどますます面白くなる。means, "The more I hear, the more interesting it becomes." This grammar is often paired with ますます which means "increasingly" and just further strengthens the statement.

However, before we can understand 見れば見るほど美しい顔をしています, we have to realize that 見れば見るほど美しい is a modifier of 顔 and remember that 美しい顔をする means, "to have a beautiful face." Armed with that knowledge, it should be clear that this phrase means, "the more you look, the more beautiful a face he has."

Following this, comes another similar bit of grammar that can sometimes be difficult. To break it down, we have a sentence, 恐ろしい鬼を倒す followed by ほど followed by the adjective 強い. (And this whole phrase modifies the noun 若者.) The word ほど means "extent" or "degree," but when it's followed by an adjective as it is here, it's best to think of it as meaning, "so (adjective) that…" For example, an interesting phrase in Japanese is, 目が回るほどいそがしい, which means, "I am so busy that my eyes are whirling." (We would probably more commonly say, "my head is spinning" in English.) So we can see that 恐ろしい鬼を倒すほど強い means, "He was so strong he defeats terrifying ogres" or as translated, "strong enough to defeat terrifying ogres."

ネズミの相撲

　昔々、山の近くに、貧しいけれど心のやさしいおじいさんとおばあさんが住んでいました。
　ある日のこと、おじいさんがいつものように杉を伐りに家の裏にある山へ行くと、
　「ハッケヨイ！」
　と、向こうの林の中から、おかしな声が聞こえてきます。

　「はて、誰なんだろう？妙な声だな」
　おじいさんは不思議に思いながら、そっと林の中へ入っていきました。のぞいてみると、小さな空き地にやせたネズミと太ったネズミが相撲をとっていました。
　「ほほう、これは面白い」
　おじいさんは木の陰に隠れて、見ていました。
　「おら、うちのやせたネズミだ！」
　やせたネズミはおじいさんの家のネズミで、太ったネズミは村の金持ちの家のネズミです。
　「がんばれ、がんばれ！」
　おじいさんはいっしょうけんめい応援をしました。
　けれども、おじいさんの家に住んでいるネズミは力が弱くて、何度やっても太ったネズミに負けてしまいます。
　おじいさんは、自分の家のやせたネズミがかわいそうになりました。

　家に帰ると、おばあさんにネズミの話をしました。
　「あれ、かわいそうだな。私は涙が出たわ。いくらかかっていっても、投げられて、泥だらけになってな。なんとかして、うちのやせたネズミに勝たせてやりたいねえ」
　「わしもそうしてやりたいが、うちは貧乏でおいしい食べ物などないし」
　おじいさんはフウッと息を吐きました。
　するとおばあさんが、
　「それでは、おモチを作って、うちのやせたネズミに食べさせてやりましょうよ。きっと、力がつきますよ」
　と、言いました。
　そこで、二人はお正月のために大事にしまってあるお米を炊いて、おモチをつきました。
　おじいさんとおばあさんはおモチを団子に丸めて、ネズミがよく顔を出す棚の上に置きました。
　「さあ、ここに置いておくよ。たくさん食べて、力をつけるんだよ」

　次の日の朝、おモチは全部なくなっていました。
　「よし。よし。これで、うんと力がついただろう」
　おじいさんは喜びながら、また山へ出かけていきました。

　そして、杉を伐りながら、おかしな声が聞こえてきます。

　「デンカショッ、　デンカショッ」
　昨日と同じようにネズミたちの掛け声が聞こえてきました。おじいさんはニコニコ林の中へ入っていきました。やせたネズミと太ったネズミは、また相撲をとりました。
　「ヨイトマケ」
　金持ちの家の太ったネズミが、足を上げて、地面を踏みました。
　「ヨイトマケ」
　おじいさんの家のネズミも力いっぱい地面を踏みました。

　二匹のネズミは組み合いましたが、金持ちの家のネズミ
が投げ飛ばされてしまいました。
　「よし。もう一度！」
　でも、今日はおじいさんの家のやせたネズミが、何度や
っても相撲に勝つのです。投げ飛ばされるのは、いつも金持
ちの家の太ったネズミです。
　不思議に思った太ったズミが、やせたネズミに首をかし
げながら尋ねました。
　「おかしいな。お前、どうして急に強くなったんだい？」

　やせたネズミは、腕を自慢に見せながら、言いました。
　「えへへへっ、じつはね。ゆうべうんとモチ食ったから、
力が強くなったんだ」
　「いいなあ、ぼくの家はお金持ちだけど、ケチだからお
モチなんか作ってくれないんだ」
　「それなら、家へおいでよ。おじいさんはきっと今夜も
おモチをついてくれるから、君にも半分わけてあげるよ」
　「本当に！うれしいなあ」
　それを聞いたおじいさんは
　「全部お米を炊いて、二匹のネズミにいっぱいおモチを
食べさせてやりましょう。お正月はまだずっと先のこと。ど
うにかなりますよ」
　と、またおモチをついて、ネズミがよく顔を出す棚の上
に二匹分置いてやりました。やさしいおばあさんは二匹のネ
ズミに赤いまわしをぬってあげて、おモチのわきに置きまし
た。
　家に帰った二匹のネズミは、おモチとまわしを見つけて
大喜びです。

　朝起きると、おモチもまわしもなくなっていました。
　「ばあさん、ゆうべはお金持ちの家のネズミが来たよう
だな。さて、今日はどっちが勝つかな」
　おじいさんはわくわくしながら、山へ出かけようとしま
した。すると、家の隅に金の硬貨は三つ置いてあることに気

付きました。喜んだ太ったネズミはおみやげに持ってきた硬貨をおじいさんとおばあさんにあげたんです。

「ばあさん！お金持ちの家のネズミは本当にお宝を持ってきたよ」

おじいさんはビックリして、おばあさんを呼びました。

おじいさんはおばあさんを連れて、山へ出かけていきました。

「デンカショッ、　デンカショッ」

いつもより、元気な声が聞こえてきました。

「それ、それ、始まった。見に行こう」

おじいさんはおばあさんの手を引いて、林の中へ入っていきました。赤いまわしを締めたかわいいネズミが組んだり離れたりして、相撲をとっています。けれども、どちらも強くて、何度やっても、勝負はつきません。

おじいさんとおばあさんは楽しそうに夕方までネズミの相撲を見ていました。

それから、おじいさんとおばあさんはお金持ちの家のネズミが持ってきた金で、いつまでも幸せに暮らしたそうです。

THE MICE'S SUMO

Long ago, a poor but kind-hearted old man and woman lived near a mountain.

One day, the old man went to the mountain behind his house to cut down cedars as usual and heard a strange voice coming from inside the woods across the way say, "Match!"

"My, who could it be? That's a strange voice."

The old man wondered and quietly went into the woods. When he took a peek, a skinny mouse and a fat mouse were sumo wrestling in a small clearing.

"Ho-ho, this is amusing."

The old man hid himself behind a tree and watched.

"Oh, it's the skinny mouse from my home!"

The skinny mouse was a mouse from the old man's home and the fat mouse was a mouse from the home of a rich man in town.

"Hang in there! Go for it!" The old man cheered with all his might.

But the mouse that lived in the old man's home had no strength and no matter how many times they wrestled, he lost to the fat mouse.

The old man came to feel sorry for the skinny mouse from his home.

When he returned home, he told the old woman about the mouse.

"Oh, that's pitiful, isn't it? It brings me to tears. No matter how much he goes at the other mouse, he is thrown and gets covered in mud. Somehow or other, I want to make our skinny mouse win."

"I also want to do so, but since we are poor, we have no delicious food or anything, so…"

The old man sighed, expelling a long breath.

Then the old woman said,

"Well then, I will make *mochi* and feed it to our skinny mouse. That will certainly give him strength."

So the couple cooked the rice they had carefully stored away for New Years, and pounded it into *mochi*.

The old man and the old woman rolled the *mochi* into dumplings and placed them on the shelf where the mouse often showed his face.

"Let's see, I'll put it here for him. Eating a lot will build his strength."

The next morning, the *mochi* was completely gone.

"Good, good. With this, his strength will have increased for sure."

The old man joyfully left for the mountain again.

And, while he was cutting cedars down, he heard the strange voices.

"Heigh-ho! Heigh-ho!"

The same as yesterday, he heard the mice's enthusiastic shouts. With a smile, the old man went into the woods. The skinny mouse and the fat mouse were sumo wrestling again.

"Heave-ho!"

The fat mouse from the rich man's home lifted its leg and stamped the ground.

"Heave-ho!"

The mouse from the old man's home also stamped the ground powerfully.

The two mice grappled and the mouse from the rich man's house was tossed.

"Alright. Once again!"

But today, the skinny mouse from the old man's home won at sumo no matter how many times they wrestled. The one who was thrown was always the fat mouse from the rich man's home.

The puzzled fat mouse tilted his head to the side and asked the skinny mouse.

"This is strange. How did you suddenly become strong?"

The skinny mouse proudly displayed his arms and said, "Ehehehe, to tell you the truth, last night I ate lots of *mochi*, so I became strong."

"Nice! I live in a rich man's house, but they're stingy and don't make me anything like *mochi*."

"In that case, come to my house. Surely the old man will pound *mochi* for me tonight, so I'll split it with you."

"Really!? I'm so glad."

When he heard this, the old man said, "We'll cook all the rice and let the two mice eat their fill. New Year's is still a long way off. We'll manage one way or another." And again they pounded *mochi* and laid out two servings for the mice on the shelf where the mouse often showed his face. The kind old woman sewed red loincloths for the two mice and placed them next to the *mochi*.

When they returned to the house, the two mice found the *mochi* and loincloths and were overjoyed.

When they woke in the morning, both the *mochi* and the loincloths were gone.

"Grandma, it seems that the mouse from the rich man's home came last night. Well, I wonder which of them will win."

Excited, the old man was about to head out to the mountain. And then he noticed, in the corner of the house, three gold coins had been set in a pile. These were coins the delighted fat mouse had brought as a present to give to the old man and woman.

"Grandma! The mouse from the rich man's house truly brought a treasure," the old man called to the old woman in surprise.

The old man took the old woman along and left for the mountain.

"Heigh-ho! Heigh-ho!"

The voices they heard were more energetic than usual.

"There, there, it's begun. Let's go watch."

The old man led the old woman by the hand and went into the woods. The cute mice, wrapped in their red loincloths, sumo wrestled, grappling and separating. But both were strong and no matter how many times they went at it, the match couldn't be decided.

The old man and the old woman watched the mice's sumo cheerfully until evening.

After that, with the money the mouse from the rich man's house brought, the old man and the old woman lived happily ever after.

VOCABULARY AND GLOSS

　昔々、山の近くに、貧しいけれど心のやさしいおじいさんとおばあさんが住んでいました。
　ある日のこと、おじいさんがいつものように杉を伐りに家の裏にある山へ行くと、
　「ハッケヨイ！」
　と、向こうの林の中から、おかしな声が聞こえてきます。

貧しい【まずしい】Poor, needy
心【こころ】のやさしい　Kind-hearted
いつものように　Like always
杉【すぎ】Cedar tree
伐る【きる】To cut down
家【いえ】House, home
裏【うら】Behind
ハッケヨイ　The match is over!
向こう【むこう】Other side, over there
林【はやし】Woods, forest
おかしい　Strange
声【こえ】Voice
聞こえる【きこえる】Is audible

ハッケヨイ is a sumo term that the referee shouts when the wrestling has come to an end. There are a few sumo yells in this story, which are in katakana.

「はて、誰なんだろう？妙な声だな」
　おじいさんは不思議に思いながら、そっと林の中へ入っていきました。のぞいてみると、小さな空き地にやせたネズミと太ったネズミが相撲をとっていました。
　「ほほう、これは面白い」
　おじいさんは木の陰に隠れて、見ていました。
　「おら、うちのやせたネズミだ！」

はて　　My, Dear me
妙【みょう】Unusual, strange
不思議【ふしぎ】Strange, mysterious
そっと　　Quietly, secretly
入る【はいる】To enter
のぞく　　To peek into
空き地【あきち】Vacant land
やせる　　To become thin
ネズミ　　Mouse
太る【ふとる】To become fat
相撲【すもう】Sumo
とる　　To compete
面白い【おもしろい】Amusing
木【き】Tree
陰【かげ】Other side, behind
隠れる【かくれる】To conceal oneself
うち　　Home, household (one's own)

Both 陰 and 影 mean "shadow" (and have the same pronunciation), but 陰 refers to places that are hidden from direct light or the line of sight of an observer. For example, 人の陰で悪口を言うな means, "Don't speak ill of others behind their backs."

　やせたネズミはおじいさんの家のネズミで、太ったネズミは村の金持ちの家のネズミです。
　「がんばれ、がんばれ！」
　おじいさんはいっしょうけんめい応援をしました。
　けれども、おじいさんの家に住んでいるネズミは力が弱くて、何度やっても太ったネズミに負けてしまいます。

村【むら】Village
金持ち【かねもち】Rich person
がんばる　Go for it, Do one's best
いっしょうけんめい　With all one's might
応援【おうえん】Cheering
力【ちから】Might, strength
弱い【よわい】Weak
何度【なんど】How many times
やる　To do, perform
負ける【まける】To lose, be defeated

Cultural Note:

The term 一生懸命【いっしょうけんめい】was originally written 一所懸命【いっしょけんめい】and referred to samurai risking their lives to defend their ancestral homes. 一所 means "one place" or "the same place" and 懸命 means, "risking one's life." The modern spelling has changed to 一生懸命, and the meaning can also be toned down a little to just mean "very hard" or "with utmost effort."

　おじいさんは、自分の家のやせたネズミがかわいそうに
なりました。
　家に帰ると、おばあさんにネズミの話をしました。
　「あれ、かわいそうだな。私は涙が出たわ。いくらかか
っていっても、投げられて、泥だらけになってな。なんとか
して、うちのやせたネズミに勝たせてやりたいねえ」

かわいそう　　Pitiable, poor
話【はなし】をする　　To tell a story
あれ　　Eh?
涙【なみだ】Tear
出る【でる】To come forth, appear
いくら　　How much?
かかる　　To go at
投げる【なげる】To throw
泥【どろ】Mud
〜だらけ　　Covered all over
なんとかして　　In one way or another
勝つ【かつ】To win

The particle わ is added to the ends of statements to soften them and make them seem less assertive. In standard Japanese (the Japanese spoken in Tokyo), it is almost always used by women, but it seems to vary depending on the region. (The masculine/feminine speech patterns of Japanese are not as clear cut as textbooks make them out to be.)

だらけ is a suffix added to nouns to mean that the subject is "covered with" or "full of" the modified noun. However, the modified noun is usually something negative like mistakes or mud or something. For example, テーブルはほこりだらけだ means, "The table is covered with dust."

「わしもそうしてやりたいが、うちは貧乏でおいしい食べ物などないし」

おじいさんはフウッと息を吐きました。

するとおばあさんが、

「それでは、おモチを作って、うちのやせたネズミに食べさせてやりましょうよ。きっと、力がつきますよ」

わし　I (used by older men)
貧乏【びんぼう】Poor, destitute
おいしい　Delicious
食べ物【たべもの】Food
フウ　Blowing sound
息【いき】Breath
吐く【つく】To exhale
それでは　Well then
おモチ　Mochi, rice cakes
作る【つくる】To make
力がつく　Gain strength
そこで　So, accordingly

The word うち means "home, household," but can also be used to mean "my" or "our." For example, うちの子供は学校にいます means, "My children are in school."

When し comes at the end of a phrase, it is used to note one of several reasons for something. By using し instead of から, the old man is implying that there are other (unstated) reasons they won't be able to help the mouse win besides the fact that they are poor and don't have any delicious food.

Cultural Note:

Mochi is a gluey substance made from rice and rolled into small balls. It is often sold in ice cream shops and cafes, but is also a traditional food eaten to celebrate New Year's. Since mochi itself is bland, it is frequently stuffed with a sweet filling. This is the same mochi from Kasajizou.

　そこで、二人はお正月のために大事にしまってあるお米を炊いて、おモチをつきました。
　おじいさんとおばあさんはおモチを団子に丸めて、ネズミがよく顔を出す棚の上に置きました。
　「さあ、ここに置いておくよ。たくさん食べて、力をつけるんだよ」

二人【ふたり】Couple, two people
お正月【おしょうがつ】New Year's
大事【だいじ】Important, valuable
しまう　To put away
お米【おこめ】Rice (uncooked)
炊く【たく】To cook, boil
つく　To hit, strike
団子【だんご】Dumpling
丸める【まるめる】To make round
よく　Often
顔【かお】Face
出す【だす】To reveal, show
棚【たな】Shelf
置く【おく】
さあ　Let's see
たくさん　A lot
力をつける　To get stronger

The auxiliary verb ておく is similar to てある but instead of describing an action that results in a lasting state, it denotes an activity to prepare for something. For example, 約束【やくそく】をしておいた means, "I made a reservation (in advance)."

次の日の朝、おモチは全部なくなっていました。
「よし。よし。これで、うんと力がついただろう」
おじいさんは喜びながら、また山へ出かけていきました。

そして、杉を伐りながら、またおかしな声が聞こえてきます。
「デンカショッ、　デンカショッ」
昨日と同じようにネズミたちの掛け声が聞こえてきました。おじいさんはニコニコ林の中へ入っていきました。やせたネズミと太ったネズミは、また相撲をとりました。
「ヨイトマケ」
金持ちの家の太ったネズミが、足を上げて、地面を踏みました。
「ヨイトマケ」
おじいさんの家のネズミも力いっぱい地面を踏みました。

次【つぎ】Next
全部【ぜんぶ】All
喜ぶ【よろこぶ】Is glad
出かける【でかける】To go out, depart
デンカショッ　*See below
と同じ【おなじ】ように　Just like
掛け声【かけごえ】Enthusiastic shouts
ニコニコ Smiling (friendly)
ヨイトマケ　*See below
足【あし】Foot, leg
上げる【あげる】To raise, lift
地面【じめん】The ground
踏む【ふむ】To step on
いっぱい　Full, lots of

There are several interjections in this story that have no specific meaning. They are just 掛け声: shouts used to encourage some activity, like "Heave ho!" etc. They can also be shouts from audience members at a concert, etc.

91

　二匹のネズミは組み合いましたが、金持ちの家のネズミが投げ飛ばされてしまいました。
　「よし。もう一度！」
　でも、今日はおじいさんの家のやせたネズミが、何度やっても相撲に勝つのです。投げ飛ばされるのは、いつも金持ちの家の太ったネズミです。
　不思議に思った太ったズミが、やせたネズミに首をかしげながら尋ねました。
　「おかしいな。お前、どうして急に強くなったんだい？」

二匹【にひき】Two animals
組み合う【くみあう】To grapple with
投げ飛ばす【なげとばす】To hurl away
もう一度【おういちど】Once more
首【くび】Head, neck
かしげる　To tilt, lean
尋ねる【たずねる】To ask, inquire
お前【おまえ】You (informal)
急に【きゅうに】Suddenly
強い【つよい】Strong
だい　Wh-question particle

The auxiliary verb 合う can be attached to a verb to give the meaning, "to do (verb) to each other" or "to do (verb) together." For example, 話し合う means, "to talk together" and 知り合う means, "to get to know (someone)."

やせたネズミは、腕を自慢に見せながら、言いました。
「えへへへっ、じつはね。ゆうべうんとモチ食ったから、力が強くなったんだ」
「いいなあ、ぼくの家はお金持ちだけど、ケチだからおモチなんか作ってくれないんだ」
「それなら、家へおいでよ。おじいさんはきっと今夜もおモチをついてくれるから、君にも半分わけてあげるよ」

腕【うで】Arm
自慢【じまん】Pride
見せる【みせる】To show
じつは　In fact, to tell the truth
ゆうべ　Last night
うんと　A lot, a great deal
食う【くう】To eat (vulgar)
ぼく　I (informal)
ケチ　Stingy
なんか　Or something
それなら　If that's the case
おいで　Come (imperative)
きっと　Surely, almost certainly (90%)
今夜【こんや】Tonight
君【きみ】You (informal)
半分【はんぶん】Half
わける　To divide, share

ゆうべ is the conversational form of "last night." You are more likely to hear this in conversations than さくや.

おいで is a colloquial way to use "come" (or "go") as an imperative.

「本当に！うれしいなあ」
それを聞いたおじいさんは
「全部お米を炊いて、二匹のネズミにいっぱいおモチを食べさせてやりましょう。お正月はまだずっと先のこと。どうにかなりますよ」
と、またおモチをついて、ネズミがよく顔を出す棚の上に二匹分置いてやりました。やさしいおばあさんは二匹のネズミに赤いまわしをぬってあげて、おモチのわきに置きました。
家に帰った二匹のネズミは、おモチとまわしを見つけて大喜びです。

本当に【ほんとうに】Really
うれしい　Glad
聞く【きく】To hear
まだ　Still
ずっと　Far away
先【さき】The future, ahead
どうにか　One way or another
二匹分【にひきぶん】Two (animals') portions
赤い【あかい】Red
まわし　Loincloth
ぬう　To sew
わき　Beside, nearby
見つける【みつける】To find, come across
大喜び【おおよろこび】Great joy

　朝起きると、おモチもまわしもなくなっていました。
　「ばあさん、ゆうべはお金持ちの家のネズミが来たよう
だな。さて、今日はどっちが勝つかな」
　おじいさんはわくわくしながら、山へ出かけようとしま
した。すると、家の隅に金の硬貨は三つ置いてあることに気
付きました。喜んだ太ったネズミはおみやげに持ってきた硬
貨をおじいさんとおばあさんにあげたんです。
　「ばあさん！お金持ちの家のネズミは本当にお宝を持っ
てきたよ」
　おじいさんはビックリして、おばあさんを呼びました。

朝【あさ】Morning
起きる【おきる】To wake up
よう　　Seems, appears
さて　　Well
どっち　　Which (informal)
わくわく　　Excited
隅【すみ】Corner
金【きん】Gold
硬貨【こうか】Coin
三つ【みっつ】Three
気付く【きづく】To notice
おみやげ　　Present, souvenir
持ってくる【もってくる】To bring
宝【たから】A treasure
ビックリ　　Surprise
呼ぶ【よぶ】To call

We have previously seen, in The Child Rearing Ghost, that the
volitional form of a verb followed by とする give the meaning of
"make an effort to do." This sometimes is better translated as
"about to do" depending on the context. From the story, we have,
山へ出かけようとしました. So the old man is "making an
effort" to head out to the mountain, but before he does that, he
notices the gold coins.

　おじいさんはおばあさんを連れて、山へ出かけていきました。
　「デンカショッ、　デンカショッ」
　いつもより、元気な声が聞こえてきました。
　「それ、それ、始まった。見に行こう」
　おじいさんはおばあさんの手を引いて、林の中へ入っていきました。赤いまわしを締めたかわいいネズミが組んだり離れたりして、相撲をとっています。けれども、どちらも強くて、何度やっても、勝負はつきません。
　おじいさんとおばあさんは楽しそうに夕方までネズミの相撲を見ていました。
　それから、おじいさんとおばあさんはお金持ちの家のネズミが持ってきた金で、いつまでも幸せに暮らしたそうです。

連れる【つれる】To take (person) along
いつもより　More than usual
始まる【はじまる】To begin
手を引く【ひく】To lead by the hand
締める【しめる】To tie, fasten
組む【くむ】To grapple, wrestle
離れる【はなれる】To separate
どちらも　Both
勝負【しょうぶ】Victory or defeat
夕方【ゆうがた】Evening
金【かね】Money
いつまでも　Forever
幸せ【しあわせ】Happy
暮らす【くらす】To live, get along

お握りコロリン

　昔々、おじいさんとおばあさんがいました。ある日、おじいさんは、おばあさんに大きなお握りを作ってもらい、山へ木を伐りに出かけました。

　トンカントンカン木を伐っているうちにお昼になりました。

　「さて、お腹が空いた」

　おじいさんは草に座って、お弁当を食べることにしました。お握りの包みを開けました。その途端、お握りがコロリンと地面に落ちて、コロコロ転がりました。おじいさんは慌ててお握りを追いかけました。お握りはコロコロ転がって、コロリン穴の中に落ちました。

　「困ったな」

　おじいさんは中をのぞきました。すると、かわいいネズミが出てきて、

　「おじいさん、お握りありがとう」と言いました。

　「なんてかわいいネズミだ」

　おじいさんはお握りを忘れてネズミを見つめました。

　「お礼に俺たちの国へ案内します」

　「でも、こんな小さな穴には入れない」

　「大丈夫。俺の尻尾につかまって、目を閉じてください」

　おじいさんはネズミの尻尾をつかんで、目を閉じました。すると、おじいさんはお握りのようにコロコロ転がりながら、穴の中へ入っていきました。
　「はあい、目を開けて」
　とネズミが言いました。ハッとして目を開けたら、屋敷のような家があって、広い台所で大勢のネズミたちがおモチをついていました。
　ネズミたちはおモチをつきながら、声を合わせて歌いました。
　『百になっても二百になっても猫の声は聞きたくない
　子供の代になっても孫の代になっても猫の声は聞きたくない』
　おじいさんがニコニコして見ているとさっきのネズミが出てきて、おじいさんを座敷に連れていきました。ネズミたちはおモチをどんどん運んできて、
　「さあ、食え、食え」
　と言いました。
　おじいさんはお腹の皮が破れるほどおモチを食べました。

　「そろそろ帰らなくちゃ」
　おじいさんが言ったら、ネズミたちはおモチと一緒に籠の中の金の硬貨をいっぱいくれました。
　「おじいさん、お握りをありがとう。これはおみやげです」
　おじいさんがネズミの尻尾につかまると、いつのまにか自分の家の前に立っていました。

　さて、この話を聞いた欲張りなじいさんは、
　「わしもネズミの穴へ行ってくる」
　と言って大きなお握りを作り、山へ出かけました。
　「ここだ、ここだ」
　おじいさんは穴を見つけると、中へお握りを投げ込みました。
　「早く出てこい」

　おじいさんがイライラして待っていたら、かわいいネズミが出てきました。
　「おじいさん、お握り、ありがとう」
　「お礼なんか言わなくてもいい。早くネズミの屋敷へ連れて行け」
　おじいさんは、いきなりネズミの尻尾をつかんで目を閉じました。
　いつのまにか、目を開けると屋敷のような家があり、広い台所で大勢のネズミたちが歌いながらおモチをついていました。
　『百になっても二百になっても猫の声は聞きたくない
　子供の代になっても孫の代になっても猫の声は聞きたくない』
　（猫がとても怖がっているように見える。）
　おじいさんはニヤッと笑うと、座敷へ入りました。
　（どのくらい硬貨をくれるかな。）
　おじいさんは床の間の籠ばかり見つめていました。
　（そうだ。猫の鳴き声をすればいい。ネズミたちが逃げたら、籠の硬貨は俺のもの。）
　おじいさんは思い切り声を出して、
　『ニャオウ！』
　と言いました。途端に辺りが真っ暗になり、ネズミたちが逃げていきました。
　「うまく行った！」
　おじいさんは手探りで籠を開け、硬貨をポケットに押し込みました。
　ところが、どっちへ行ったらいいのか、出口がわかりません。おじいさんは暗い穴の中を行ったり来たり、帰る道を見つけることはできません。

VOCABULARY

お握り【おにぎり】Rice ball
伐る【きる】To cut down (tree)
出かける【でかける】To depart, set out
トンカン　Chopping sound
うちに　While
お昼【おひる】Noon, lunch
さて　Now, well, then
お腹【おなか】Stomach
空く【すく】Is empty
お腹が空く　To be hungry
草【くさ】Grass
座る【すわる】To sit
お弁当【おべんとう】Bento, boxed lunch
包み【つつみ】Package
開ける【あける】To open
途端【とたん】Just then
コロリン　Slip and fall sound
地面【じめん】The ground
コロコロ　Rolling sound
転がる【ころがる】To roll, tumble
慌てる【あわてる】To be in a rush
追いかける【おいかける】To chase after

穴【あな】A hole
困る【こまる】To be troubled, at a loss
のぞく　To peek into
すると　Hereupon
ネズミ　Mouse
なんて　What…?　How…?
お礼【おれい】Thanks, gratitude
俺【おれ】I (informal male)
国【くに】Home, country
案内【あんない】To guide, show around
入る【はいる】To enter
尻尾【しっぽ】Tail
つかまる　To hold on to, grasp
目【め】Eyes
閉じる【とじる】To close
ハッと　Taken aback, surprised
屋敷【やしき】Mansion
広い【ひろい】Wide
台所【だいどころ】Kitchen
大勢【おおぜい】A large crowd
声【こえ】Voices
合わせる【あわせる】To unite
歌う【うたう】To sing
百【ひゃく】Hundred
猫【ねこ】Cat
聞く【きく】To hear
子供【こども】Child
代【だい】Generation
孫【まご】Grandchild
さっき　Just a minute ago
座敷【ざしき】Tatami room
連れる【つれる】To lead, take along
どんどん　Rapidly, steadily
運ぶ【はこぶ】To carry

さあ　Go on
食う【くう】To eat (vulgar)
食え（Imperative form of 食う）
皮【かわ】Shell, wrapping, rind
破れる【やぶれる】To get torn, rip
そろそろ　Soon, any time now
一緒に【いっしょに】Together
籠【かご】Basket
金【きん】Gold
硬貨【こうか】Coin
いっぱい　A lot, full
おみやげ　Present, souvenir
いつのまにか　Before one knows it
立つ【たつ】To stand
話【はなし】Story
欲張り【よくばり】Greed
見つける【みつける】To find
投げ込む【なげこむ】To throw into
こい（Imperative form of 来る）
イライラする　Gets irritated
行け（Imperative form of 行く）
いきなり　Abruptly, without warning
つかむ　To grasp, hold
怖い【こわい】Scary
見える【みえる】To seem, appear
笑う【わらう】To smile
ニヤッと笑う　To grin
どのくらい　How much
床の間【とこのま】Alcove where decorations are displayed
ばかり　Just, only
見つめる【みつめる】To stare, gaze at
鳴き声【なきごえ】Meow, cry
すればいい　All I have to do is
逃げる【にげる】To escape, run away

思い切り【おもいきり】With all one's might
声を出す　To vocalize, speak
辺り【あたり】Vicinity
真っ暗【まっくら】Pitch black
うまく　Smoothly, well, skillfully
うまく行く　To go well
手探り【てさぐり】Fumbling, groping
ポケット　Pocket
押し込む【おしこむ】To stuff into
ところが　However
たらいい　Should
出口【でぐち】Exit
暗い【くらい】Dark
道【みち】Way, road

www.ingramcontent.com/pod-product-compliance
Lightning Source LLC
Chambersburg PA
CBHW031137250726
48655CB00002B/708